Harvard
Business
Review

ON

DECISION MAKING

THE HARVARD BUSINESS REVIEW PAPERBACK SERIES

The series is designed to bring today's managers and professionals the fundamental information they need to stay competitive in a fast-moving world. From the preeminent thinkers whose work has defined an entire field to the rising stars who will redefine the way we think about business, here are the leading minds and landmark ideas that have established the *Harvard Business Review* as required reading for ambitious businesspeople in organizations around the globe.

Other books in the series:

Harvard Business Review Interviews with CEOs

Harvard Business Review on Brand Management

Harvard Business Review on Breakthrough Thinking

Harvard Business Review on Business and the Environment

Harvard Business Review on the Business Value of IT

Harvard Business Review on Change

Harvard Business Review on Corporate Governance

Harvard Business Review on Corporate Strategy

Harvard Business Review on Crisis Management

Harvard Business Review on Effective Communication

Harvard Business Review on Entrepreneurship

Harvard Business Review on Finding and Keeping the Best People

Harvard Business Review on Knowledge Management

Harvard Business Review on Leadership

Harvard Business Review on Managing High-Tech Industries

Harvard Business Review on Managing People

Harvard Business Review on Managing Uncertainty

Harvard Business Review on Managing the Value Chain

Other books in the series (continued):

Harvard Business Review on Measuring Corporate Performance

Harvard Business Review on Mergers and Acquisitions

Harvard Business Review on Negotiation and Conflict Resolution

Harvard Business Review on Nonprofits

Harvard Business Review on Strategies for Growth

Harvard Business Review on Work and Life Balance

Harvard Business Review

ON

DECISION MAKING

The *Harvard Business Review* articles in this collection are available as
individual reprints. Discounts apply to quantity purchases. For information and ordering, please contact Customer Service, Harvard Business
School Publishing, Boston, MA 02163. Telephone: (617) 783-7500 or
(800) 988-0886, 8 A.M. to 6 P.M. Eastern Time, Monday through Friday.
Fax: (617) 783-7555, 24 hours a day. E-mail: custserv@hbsp.harvard.edu.

978-1-57851-557-8 (ISBN 13)

Library of Congress Cataloging-in-Publication Data
Harvard business review on decision making.
       p.   cm. — (Harvard business review paperback series)
    Includes index.
    ISBN 1-57851-557-2
    1. Decision making.   I. Title: On decision making.   II. Title: Deci-
sion making.   III. Harvard business review.   IV. Series.
HD30.23 .H374 2001
658.4′03—dc21   00-052986
                                                              CIP

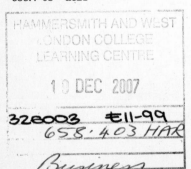

326003

Contents

The Effective Decision   1
PETER F. DRUCKER

Even Swaps:
A Rational Method for Making Trade-offs   21
JOHN S. HAMMOND, RALPH L. KEENEY, AND HOWARD RAIFFA

Humble Decision Making   45
AMITAI ETZIONI

Interpersonal Barriers to Decision Making   59
CHRIS ARGYRIS

Can You Analyze This Problem?   97
PERRIN STRYKER

How to Analyze That Problem:
Part II of a Management Exercise   113
PERRIN STRYKER

The Hidden Traps in Decision Making   143
JOHN S. HAMMOND, RALPH L. KEENEY, AND HOWARD RAIFFA

When to Trust Your Gut   169
ALDEN M. HAYASHI

About the Contributors   189

Index   193

Harvard
Business
Review

ON

DECISION MAKING

The Effective Decision

PETER F. DRUCKER

Executive Summary

THE RISK-TAKING JUDGMENTS that an executive must make are infrequent but crucial; they can be better understood if broken down into six sequential steps.

EFFECTIVE EXECUTIVES do not make a great many decisions. They concentrate on what is important. They try to make the few important decisions on the highest level of conceptual understanding. They try to find the constants in a situation, to think through what is strategic and generic rather than to "solve problems." They are, therefore, not overly impressed by speed in decision making; rather, they consider virtuosity in manipulating a great many variables a symptom of sloppy thinking. They want to know what the

1

decision is all about and what the underlying realities
are which it has to satisfy. They want impact rather
than technique. And they want to be sound rather than
clever.

Effective executives know when a decision has to be
based on principle and when it should be made pragmatically, on the merits of the case. They know the trickiest
decision is that between the right and the wrong compromise, and they have learned to tell one from the
other. They know that the most time-consuming step in
the process is not making the decision but putting it into
effect. Unless a decision has degenerated into work, it is
not a decision; it is at best a good intention. This means
that, while the effective decision itself is based on the
highest level of conceptual understanding, the action
commitment should be as close as possible to the capacities of the people who have to carry it out. Above all,
effective executives know that decision making has its
own systematic process and its own clearly defined elements.

Sequential Steps

The elements do not by themselves "make" the decisions.
Indeed, every decision is a risk-taking judgment. But
unless these elements are the stepping stones of the decision process, the executive will not arrive at a right, and
certainly not at an effective, decision. Therefore, in this
article I shall describe the sequence of steps involved in
the decision-making process.

1. **Classifying the problem.** Is it generic? Is it exceptional and unique? Or is it the first manifestation of a
new genus for which a rule has yet to be developed?

2. **Defining the problem.** What are we dealing with?

3. **Specifying the answer to the problem.** What are the "boundary conditions"?

4. **Deciding what is "right," rather than what is acceptable, in order to meet the boundary conditions.** What will fully satisfy the specifications *before* attention is given to the compromises, adaptations, and concessions needed to make the decision acceptable?

5. **Building into the decision the action to carry it out.** What does the action commitment have to be? Who has to know about it?

6. **Testing the validity and effectiveness of the decision against the actual course of events.** How is the decision being carried out? Are the assumptions on which it is based appropriate or obsolete?

Let us take a look at each of these individual elements.

The Classification

The effective decision maker asks: Is this a symptom of a fundamental disorder or a stray event? The generic always has to be answered through a rule, a principle. But the truly exceptional event can only be handled as such and as it comes.

Strictly speaking, the executive might distinguish among four, rather than between two, different types of occurrences.

First, there is the truly generic event, of which the individual occurrence is only a symptom. Most of the "problems" that come up in the course of the executive's

work are of this nature. Inventory decisions in a business, for instance, are not "decisions." They are adaptations. The problem is generic. This is even more likely to
be true of occurrences within manufacturing organizations. For example:

*A product control and engineering group will typically
handle many hundreds of problems in the course of a
month. Yet, whenever these are analyzed, the great
majority prove to be just symptoms—and manifestations—of underlying basic situations. The individual process control engineer or production engineer who works
in one part of the plant usually cannot see this. He might
have a few problems each month with the couplings in the
pipes that carry steam or hot liquids, and that's all.*

Only when the total workload of the group over several months is analyzed does the generic problem
appear. Then it is seen that temperatures or pressures
have become too great for the existing equipment and
that the couplings holding the various lines together
need to be redesigned for greater loads. Until this analysis is done, process control will spend a tremendous
amount of time fixing leaks without ever getting control
of the situation.

The second type of occurrence is the problem which,
while a unique event for the individual institution, is
actually generic. Consider:

*The company that receives an offer to merge from
another, larger one, will never receive such an offer again
if it accepts. This is a nonrecurrent situation as far as the
individual company, its board of directors, and its management are concerned. But it is, of course, a generic situation which occurs all the time. Thinking through*

whether to accept or to reject the offer requires some general rules. For these, however, the executive has to look to the experience of others.

Next there is the truly exceptional event that the executive must distinguish. To illustrate:

The huge power failure that plunged into darkness the whole of Northeastern North America from St. Lawrence to Washington in November 1965 was, according to first explanations, a truly exceptional situation. So was the thalidomide tragedy which led to the birth of so many deformed babies in the early 1960s. The probability of either of these events occurring, we were told, was one in ten million or one in a hundred million, and concatenations of these events were as unlikely ever to recur again as it is unlikely, for instance, for the chair on which I sit to disintegrate into its constituent atoms.

Truly unique events are rare, however. Whenever one appears, the decision maker has to ask: Is this a true exception or only the first manifestation of a new genus? And this—the early manifestation of a new generic problem—is the fourth and last category of events with which the decision process deals. Thus:

We know now that both the Northeastern power failure and the thalidomide tragedy were only the first occurrences of what, under conditions of modern power technology or of modern pharmacology, are likely to become fairly frequent occurrences unless generic solutions are found.

All events but the truly unique require a generic solution. They require a rule, a policy, or a principle. Once the right principle has been developed, all manifestations of the same generic situation can be handled pragmatically—that is, by adaptation of the rule to the concrete circumstances of the case. Truly unique events, however, must be treated individually. The executive cannot develop rules for the exceptional.

The effective decision maker spends time determining which of the four different situations is happening. The wrong decision will be made if the situation is classified incorrectly.

By far the most common mistake of the decision maker is to treat a generic situation as if it were a series of unique events—that is, to be pragmatic when lacking the generic understanding and principle. The inevitable result is frustration and futility. This was clearly shown, I think, by the failure of most of the policies, both domestic and foreign, of the Kennedy Administration. Consider:

> For all the brilliance of its members, the Administration achieved fundamentally only one success, and that was in the Cuban missile crisis. Otherwise, it achieved practically nothing. The main reason was surely what its members called "pragmatism"—namely, the Administration's refusal to develop rules and principles, and its insistence on training everything "on its merits." Yet it was clear to everyone, including the members of the Administration, that the basic assumptions on which its policies rested— the valid assumptions of the immediate postwar years— had become increasingly unrealistic in international, as well as in domestic, affairs in the 1960's.

Equally common is the mistake of treating a new event as if it were just another example of the old problem to which, therefore, the old rules should be applied:

This was the error that snowballed the local power failure on the New York–Ontario border into the great Northeastern blackout. The power engineers, especially in New York City, applied the right rule for a normal overload. Yet their own instruments had signaled that something quite extraordinary was going on which called for exceptional, rather than standard, countermeasures.

By contrast, the one great triumph of President Kennedy in the Cuban missile crisis rested on acceptance of the challenge to think through an extraordinary, exceptional occurrence. As soon as he accepted this, his own tremendous resources of intelligence and courage effectively came into play.

The Definition

Once a problem has been classified as generic or unique, it is usually fairly easy to define. "What is this all about?" "What is pertinent here?" "What is the key to this situation?" Questions such as these are familiar. But only the truly effective decision makers are aware that the danger in this step is not the wrong definition; it is the plausible but incomplete one. For example:

The American automobile industry held to a plausible but incomplete definition of the problem of automotive safety. It was this lack of awareness—far more than any reluctance to spend money on safety engineering—that eventually, in 1966, brought the industry under sudden and sharp Congressional attack for its unsafe cars and then left the industry totally bewildered by the attack. It simply is not true that the industry has paid scant attention to safety.

On the contrary, it has worked hard at safer highway engineering and at driver training, believing these to be the major areas for concern. That accidents are caused by unsafe roads and unsafe drivers is plausible enough. Indeed, all other agencies concerned with automotive safety, from the highway police to the high schools, picked the same targets for their campaigns. These campaigns have produced results. The number of accidents on highways built for safety has been greatly lessened. Similarly, safety-trained drivers have been involved in far fewer accidents.

But although the ratio of accidents per thousand cars or per thousand miles driven has been going down, the total number of accidents and the severity of them have kept creeping up. It should therefore have become clear long ago that something would have to be done about the small but significant probability that accidents will occur despite safety laws and safety training.

This means that future safety campaigns will have to be supplemented by engineering to make accidents themselves less dangerous. Whereas cars have been engineered to be safe when used correctly, they will also have to be engineered for safety when used incorrectly.

There is only one safeguard against becoming the prisoner of an incomplete definition: check it again and again against *all* the observable facts, and throw out a definition the moment it fails to encompass any of them.

Effective decision makers always test for signs that something is atypical or something unusual is happening, always asking: Does the definition explain the observed events, and does it explain all of them? They always write out what the definition is expected to make happen—for instance, make automobile accidents disappear—and then test regularly to see if this really happens. Finally, they go back and think the problem through again whenever they see something atypical, when they find unexplained phenomena, or when the course of events deviates, even in details, from expectations.

These are in essence the rules Hippocrates laid down for medical diagnosis well over 2,000 years ago. They are the rules for scientific observation first formulated by Aristotle and then reaffirmed by Galileo 300 years ago. These, in other words, are old, well-known, time-tested rules, which an executive can learn and apply systematically.

The Specifications

The next major element in the decision process is defining clear specifications as to what the decision has to accomplish. What are the objectives the decision has to reach? What are the minimum goals it has to attain? What are the conditions it has to satisfy? In science these are known as "boundary conditions." A decision, to be effective, needs to satisfy the boundary conditions. Consider:

"Can our needs be satisfied," Alfred P. Sloan, Jr. presumably asked himself when he took command of General Motors in 1922, "by removing the autonomy of our division heads?" His answer was clearly in the negative. The boundary conditions of his problem demanded strength and responsibility in the chief operating positions. This was needed as much as unity and control at the center. Everyone before Sloan had seen the problem as one of personalities—to be solved through a struggle for power from which one man would emerge victorious. The boundary conditions, Sloan realized, demanded a

solution to a constitutional problem—to be solved
through a new structure: decentralization which balanced local autonomy of operations with central control
of direction and policy.

A decision that does not satisfy the boundary conditions is worse than one which wrongly defines the problem. It is all but impossible to salvage the decision that
starts with the right premises but stops short of the right
conclusions. Furthermore, clear thinking about the
boundary conditions is needed to know when a decision
has to be abandoned. The most common cause of failure
in a decision lies not in its being wrong initially. Rather,
it is a subsequent shift in the goals—the specifications—
which makes the prior right decision suddenly inappropriate. And unless the decision maker has kept the
boundary conditions clear, so as to make possible the
immediate replacement of the outflanked decision with
a new and appropriate policy, he may not even notice
that things have changed. For example:

> *Franklin D. Roosevelt was bitterly attacked for his switch
> from conservative candidate in 1932 to radical president
> in 1933. But it wasn't Roosevelt who changed. The sudden
> economic collapse which occurred between the summer
> of 1932 and the spring of 1933 changed the specifications.
> A policy appropriate to the goal of national economic
> recovery—which a conservative economic policy might
> have been—was no longer appropriate when, with the
> Bank Holiday, the goal had to become political and social
> cohesion. When the boundary conditions changed, Roo-
> sevelt immediately substituted a political objective
> (reform) for his former economic one (recovery).*

Above all, clear thinking about the boundary conditions is needed to identify the most dangerous of all pos-

sible decisions: the one in which the specifications that have to be satisfied are essentially incompatible. In other words, this is the decision that might—just might—work if nothing whatever goes wrong. A classic case is President Kennedy's Bay of Pigs decision:

> *One specification was clearly Castro's overthrow. The other was to make it appear that the invasion was a "spontaneous" uprising of the Cubans. But these two specifications would have been compatible with each other only if an immediate island-wide uprising against Castro would have completely paralyzed the Cuban army. And while this was not impossible, it clearly was not probable in such a tightly controlled police state.*

Decisions of this sort are usually called "gambles." But actually they arise from something much less rational than a gamble—namely, a hope against hope that two (or more) clearly incompatible specifications can be fulfilled simultaneously. This is hoping for a miracle; and the trouble with miracles is not that they happen so rarely, but that they are, alas, singularly unreliable.

Everyone can make the wrong decision. In fact, everyone will sometimes make a wrong decision. But no executive needs to make a decision which, on the face of it, seems to make sense but, in reality, falls short of satisfying the boundary conditions.

The Decision

The effective executive has to start out with what is "right" rather than what is acceptable precisely because a compromise is always necessary in the end. But if what will satisfy the boundary conditions is not known, the decision maker cannot distinguish between the right compromise and the wrong compromise—and may end up by making the wrong compromise. Consider:

> *I was taught this lesson in 1944 when I started on my first big consulting assignment. It was a study of the management structure and policies of General Motors Corporation. Alfred P. Sloan, Jr., who was then chairman and chief executive officer of the company, called me to his office at the start of my assignment and said: "I shall not tell you what to study, what to write, or what conclusions to come to. This is your task. My only instruction to you is to put down what you think is right as you see it. Don't you worry about our reaction. Don't you worry about whether we will like this or dislike that. And don't you, above all, concern yourself with the compromises that might be needed to make your conclusions acceptable. There is not one executive in this company who does not know how to make every single conceivable compromise without any help from you. But he can't make the right compromise unless you first tell him what right is."*

The effective executive knows that there are two different kinds of compromise. One is expressed in the old proverb, "Half a loaf is better than no bread." The other, in the story of the judgment of Solomon, is clearly based on the realization that "half a baby is worse than no baby at all." In the first instance, the boundary conditions are still being satisfied. The purpose of bread is to provide food, and half a loaf is still food. Half a baby, however, does not satisfy the boundary conditions. For half a baby is not half of a living and growing child.

It is a waste of time to worry about what will be acceptable and what the decision maker should or should not say so as not to evoke resistance. (The things one worries about seldom happen, while objections and difficulties no one thought about may suddenly turn out to be almost insurmountable obstacles.) In other words, the decision maker gains nothing by starting out with the question, "What is acceptable?" For in the process of answering it, he or she usually gives away the important things and loses any chance to come up with an effective—let alone the right—answer.

The Action

Converting the decision into action is the fifth major element in the decision process. While thinking through the boundary conditions is the most difficult step in decision making, converting the decision into effective action is usually the most time-consuming one. Yet a decision will not become effective unless the action commitments have been built into it from the start. In fact, no decision has been made unless carrying it out in specific steps has become someone's work assignment and responsibility. Until then, it is only a good intention.

The flaw in so many policy statements, especially those of business, is that they contain no action commitment—to carry them out is no one's specific work and responsibility. Small wonder then that the people in the organization tend to view such statements cynically, if not as declarations of what top management is really *not* going to do.

Converting a decision into action requires answering several distinct questions: Who has to know of this decision? What action has to be taken? Who is to take it? What does the action have to be so that the people who have to do it *can* do it? The first and the last of these questions are too often overlooked—with dire results. A story that has become a legend among operations researchers illustrates the importance of the question, "Who has to know?":

> *A major manufacturer of industrial equipment decided several years ago to discontinue one of its models that had for years been standard equipment on a line of machine tools, many of which were still in use. It was, therefore, decided to sell the model to present owners of the old equipment for another three years as a replacement, and then to stop making and selling it. Orders for this particular model had been going down for a good many years. But they shot up immediately as customers reordered against the day when the model would no longer be available. No one had, however, asked, "Who needs to know of this decision?"*
>
> *Consequently, nobody informed the purchasing clerk who was in charge of buying the parts from which the model itself was being assembled. His instructions were to buy parts in a given ratio to current sales—and the instructions remained unchanged.*
>
> *Thus, when the time came to discontinue further production of the model, the company had in its warehouse enough parts for another 8 to 10 years of production, parts that had to be written off at a considerable loss.*

The action must also be appropriate to the capacities of the people who have to carry it out. Thus:

> *A large U.S. chemical company found itself, in recent years, with fairly large amounts of blocked currency in two West African countries. To protect this money, top management decided to invest it locally in businesses which would: (1) contribute to the local economy, (2) not require imports from abroad, and (3) if successful, be the kind that could be sold to local investors if and when*

currency remittances became possible again. To establish these businesses, the company developed a simple chemical process to preserve a tropical fruit—a staple crop in both countries—which, up until then, had suffered serious spoilage in transit to its Western markets.

The business was a success in both countries. But in one country the local manager set the business up in such a manner that it required highly skilled and technically trained management of a kind not easily available in West Africa. In the other country, the local manager thought through the capacities of the people who would eventually have to run the business. Consequently, he worked hard at making both the process and the business simple, and at staffing his operation from the start with local nationals right up to the top management level.

A few years later it became possible again to transfer currency from these two countries. But, though the business flourished, no buyer could be found for it in the first country. No one available locally had the necessary managerial and technical skills to run it, and so the business had to be liquidated at a loss. In the other country, so many local entrepreneurs were eager to buy the business that the company repatriated its original investment with a substantial profit.

The chemical process and the business built on it were essentially the same in both places. But in the first country no one had asked, "What kind of people do we have available to make this decision effective? And what can they do?" As a result, the decision itself became frustrated.

This action commitment becomes doubly important when people have to change their behavior, habits, or attitudes if a decision is to become effective. Here, the

executive must make sure not only that the responsibility for the action is clearly assigned, but that the people
assigned are capable of carrying it out. Thus the decision
maker has to make sure that the measurements, the
standards for accomplishment, and the incentives of
those charged with the action responsibility are changed
simultaneously. Otherwise, the organization people will
get caught in a paralyzing internal emotional conflict.
Consider these two examples:

> *When Theodore Vail was president of the Bell Telephone
> System 60 years ago, he decided that its business was ser-
> vice. This decision explains in large part why the United
> States (and Canada) has today an investor-owned, rather
> than a nationalized, telephone system. Yet this policy
> statement might have remained a dead letter if Vail had
> not at the same time designed yardsticks of service per-
> formance and introduced these as a means to measure,
> and ultimately to reward, managerial performance. The
> Bell managers of that time were used to being measured
> by the profitability (or at least by the cost) of their units.
> The new yardsticks resulted in the rapid acceptance of
> the new objectives.*
>
> *In sharp contrast is the recent failure of a brilliant
> chairman and chief executive to make effective a new
> organization structure and new objectives in an old,
> large, and proud U.S. company. Everyone agreed that the
> changes were needed. The company, after many years as
> leader of its industry, showed definite signs of aging. In
> many markets newer, smaller, and more aggressive com-
> petitors were outflanking it. But contrary to the action
> required to gain acceptance for the new ideas, the chair-
> man—in order to placate the opposition—promoted
> prominent spokesmen of the old school into the most*

visible and highest salaried positions—in particular into three new executive vice presidencies. This meant only one thing to the people in the company: "They don't really mean it." If the greatest rewards are given for behavior contrary to that which the new course of action requires, then everyone will conclude that this is what the people at the top really want and are going to reward.

Only the most effective executive can do what Vail did—build the execution of his decision into the decision itself. But every executive can think through what action commitments a specific decision requires, what work assignments follow from it, and what people are available to carry it out.

The Feedback

Finally, information monitoring and reporting have to be built into the decision to provide continuous testing, against actual events, of the expectations that underlie the decisions. Decisions are made by people. People are fallible; at best, their works do not last long. Even the best decision has a high probability of being wrong. Even the most effective one eventually becomes obsolete.

This surely needs no documentation. And every executive always builds organized feedback—reports, figures, studies—into his or her decision to monitor and report on it. Yet far too many decisions fail to achieve their anticipated results, or indeed ever to become effective, despite all these feedback reports. Just as the view from the Matterhorn cannot be visualized by studying a map of Switzerland (one abstraction), a decision cannot be fully and accurately evaluated by studying a report. That is because reports are, of necessity, abstractions.

Effective decision makers know this and follow a rule which the military developed long ago. The commander who makes a decision does not depend on reports to see how it is being carried out. The commander or an aide goes and looks. The reason is not that effective decision makers (or effective commanders) distrust their subordinates. Rather, they learned the hard way to distrust abstract "communications."

With the coming of the computer this feedback element will become even more important, for the decision maker will in all likelihood be even further removed from the scene of action. Unless he or she accepts, as a matter of course, that he or she had better go out and look at the scene of action, he or she will be increasingly divorced from reality. All a computer can handle is abstractions. And abstractions can be relied on only if they are constantly checked against concrete results. Otherwise, they are certain to mislead.

To go and look is also the best, if not the only way, for an executive to test whether the assumptions on which the decision has been made are still valid or whether they are becoming obsolete and need to be thought through again. And the executive always has to expect the assumptions to become obsolete sooner or later. Reality never stands still very long.

Failure to go out and look is the typical reason for persisting in a course of action long after it has ceased to be appropriate or even rational. This is true for business decisions as well as for governmental policies. It explains in large measure the failure of Stalin's cold war policy in Europe, but also the inability of the United States to adjust its policies to the realities of a Europe restored to prosperity and economic growth, and the failure of the British to accept, until too late, the reality of the European Common Market. Moreover, in any business I know, failure to go out and look at customers and markets, at competitors and their products, is also a major reason for poor, ineffectual, and wrong decisions.

Decision makers need organized information for feedback. They need reports and figures. But unless they build their feedback around direct exposure to reality— unless they discipline themselves to go out and look— they condemn themselves to a sterile dogmatism.

Concluding Note

Decision making is only one of the tasks of an executive. It usually takes but a small fraction of his or her time. But to make the important decisions is the *specific* executive task. Only an executive makes such decisions.

An *effective* executive makes these decisions as a systematic process with clearly defined elements and in a distinct sequence of steps. Indeed, to be expected (by virtue of position or knowledge) to make decisions that have significant and positive impact on the entire organization, its performance, and its results characterizes the effective executive.

Originally published in January–February 1967
Reprint 67105

Even Swaps

A Rational Method for Making Trade-offs

JOHN S. HAMMOND, RALPH L. KEENEY,
AND HOWARD RAIFFA

Executive Summary

MAKING WISE TRADE-OFFS is one of the most important
and difficult challenges in decision making. Needless to
say, the more alternatives you're considering and the
more objectives you're pursuing, the more trade-offs
you'll need to make. The sheer volume of trade-offs, however, is not what makes decision making so hard. It's the
fact that each objective has its own basis of comparison,
from precise numbers (34% versus 38%) to relationships
(high versus low) to descriptive terms (red versus blue).
You're not just trading off apples and oranges; you're
trading off apples and oranges and elephants.

How do you make trade-offs when comparing widely
disparate things? In the past, decision makers have
relied mostly on instinct, common sense, and guesswork.
They've lacked a clear, rational, and easy-to-use trade-
off methodology. To help fill that gap, the authors have

developed a system—which they call *even swaps*—that provides a practical way of making trade-offs among a range of objectives across a range of alternatives.

The even-swap method will not make complex decisions easy; you'll still have to make hard choices about the values you set and the trades you make. What it does provide is a reliable mechanism for making the trades and a coherent framework in which to make them. By simplifying and codifying the mechanical elements of trade-offs, the even-swap method let you focus all your mental energy on the most important work of decision making: deciding the real value to your company of different courses of action.

SOME DECISIONS ARE EASY. If you want to fly from New York to San Francisco as cheaply as possible, you simply find the airline offering the lowest fare and buy a ticket. You have only a single objective, so you need to make only a single set of comparisons. But having only one objective, as any decision maker knows, is a rare luxury. Usually, you're pursuing many different objectives simultaneously. Yes, you want a low fare, but you also want a convenient departure time, a direct flight, an aisle seat, and an airline with an outstanding safety record. And you'd like to earn frequent flyer miles in one of your existing accounts. Now the decision is considerably more complicated. You have to make trade-offs.

Making wise trade-offs is one of the most important and difficult challenges in decision making. The more alternatives you're considering and the more objectives you're pursuing, the more trade-offs you'll need to make.

The sheer volume of trade-offs, though, is not what makes decision making so hard. It's the fact that each objective has its own basis of comparison. For one objective, you may compare the alternatives using precise numbers or percentages: 34%, 38%, 53%. For another objective, you may need to make broad relational judgments: high, low, medium. For another, you may use purely descriptive terms: yellow, orange, blue. You're not just trading off apples and oranges; you're trading off apples and oranges and elephants.

How do you make trade-offs when comparing such widely disparate things? In the past, decision makers have relied mostly on instinct, common sense, and guesswork. They've lacked a clear, rational, and easy-to-use trade-off methodology. To help fill that gap, we have developed a system—which we call *even swaps*—that provides a practical way of making trade-offs among any set of objectives across a range of alternatives. In essence, the even-swap method is a form of bartering—it forces you to think about the value of one objective in terms of another. How many frequent flyer miles, for example, would you sacrifice for a $50 reduction in airfare? How long would you delay your departure time to be assured an aisle seat? Once you have made such value judgments, you can make sense of the variety of different measurement systems. You have a solid, consistent basis for making sensible trade-offs.

The even-swap method will not make complex decisions easy; you'll still have to make hard choices about the values you set and the trades you make. What it does provide is a reliable mechanism for making trades and a coherent framework in which to make them. By simplifying and codifying the mechanical elements of trade-offs, the even-swap method lets you focus all your mental energy on the most important work of decision making: deciding the real value to you and your organization of different courses of action.

Creating a Consequences Table

Before you can begin making trade-offs, you need to have a clear picture of all your alternatives and their conse-quences for each of your objectives. A good way to create that picture is to draw up a *consequences table*. Using pencil and paper or a computer spreadsheet, list your objectives down the left side of a page and your alterna-tives along the top. This will give you an empty matrix. In each box of the matrix, write a concise description of the consequence that the given alternative (indicated by the column) will have for the given objective (indicated by the row). You'll likely describe some consequences in quantitative terms, using numbers, and others in qualita-tive terms, using words. The important thing is to use consistent terminology in describing all the conse-quences for a given objective; in other words, use consis-tent terms across each row. If you don't, you won't be able to make rational swaps between the objectives.

To illustrate what a consequences table actually looks like, let's examine one created by a young man we'll call Vincent Sahid. The only child of a widower, Vincent plans to take time off from college, where he's majoring in business, to help his father recover from a serious ill-ness. To make ends meet while away from school, he will need to take a job. He wants a position that pays ade-quately, has good benefits and vacation allowances, and involves enjoyable work, but he'd also like to gain some experience that will be useful when he returns to school. And, given his dad's frail condition, it is very important that the job give him the flexibility to deal with emergencies. After a lot of hard work, Vincent identifies five possible jobs. Each has very different consequences for his objectives, and he charts those consequences in a consequences table. (See "Sahid's Consequences Table.")

As we see, a consequences table puts a lot of information into a concise and orderly format that allows you to compare your alternatives easily, objective by objective. It gives you a clear framework for making trade-offs. Moreover, it imposes an important discipline, forcing you to define all alternatives, all objectives, and all relevant consequences at the outset of the decision process. Although a consequences table is not too hard to create, we're always surprised at how rarely decision makers take the time to put down on paper all the elements of a complex decision. Without a consequences table, important information can be overlooked and trade-offs can be made haphazardly, leading to wrongheaded decisions.

Eliminating "Dominated" Alternatives

Once you've defined and mapped the consequences of each alternative, you should always look for opportunities to eliminate one or more of the alternatives. The fewer the alternatives, the fewer trade-offs you'll ultimately need to make. To identify alternatives that can be eliminated, follow this simple rule: if alternative A is better than alternative B on some objectives and no worse than B on all other objectives, B can be eliminated from consideration. In such cases, B is said to be *dominated* by A—it has disadvantages without any advantages.

Say you want to take a relaxing weekend getaway. You have five places in mind, and you have three objectives: low cost, good weather, and short travel time. In looking

Sahid's Consequences Table

ALTERNATIVES

Objectives	Job A	Job B	Job C	Job D	Job E
Monthly Salary ($)	2000	2400	1800	1900	2200
Flexibility	moderate	low	high	moderate	none
Business Skills Development	computer	people management, computer	operations, computer	organization	time management, multitasking
Annual Vacation Days	14	12	10	15	12
Benefits	health, dental, retirement	health, dental	health	health, retirement	health, dental
Enjoyment	great	good	good	great	boring

at your options, you notice that alternative C costs more, has worse weather, and requires the same travel time as alternative D. Alternative C is dominated by D and therefore can be eliminated.

You need not be rigid in thinking about dominance. In making further comparisons among your options, you may find, for example, that alternative E also has higher costs and worse weather than alternative D but has a slight advantage in travel time—it would take half an hour less to get to E. You may easily conclude that the relatively small time advantage doesn't outweigh the weather and cost disadvantages. For practical purposes, alternative E is dominated—we call this *practical dominance*—and you can eliminate it as well. By looking for dominance, you have just made your decision much simpler—you only have to choose among three alternatives, not five.

A consequences table can be a great aid in identifying dominated alternatives. But if there are many alternatives and objectives, there can be so much information in the table that it gets hard to spot dominance. Glance back at Vincent Sahid's consequences table and you'll see what we mean. To make it easier to uncover dominance, you should create a second table in which the descriptions of consequences are replaced with simple rankings. Working row by row—that is, objective by objective—determine the consequence that best fulfills the objective and replace it with the number 1; then find the second-best consequence and replace it with the number 2; and continue in this way until you've ranked the consequences of all the alternatives. When Vincent looks at the vacation objective in his table, for example, he sees that 15 days ranks first, 14 days ranks second, the two 12 days tie for third, and 10 days ranks fifth. When he moves from the quantitatively measured objectives to the qualitatively measured ones, he finds that more thought is required because the rankings need to be based on subjective judgments rather than objective comparisons. In assessing the benefits packages, for example, he decides that dental coverage is more important to him than a retirement plan, and he makes his rankings on that basis. (See "Sahid's Ranking Table.")

Dominance is much easier to see when you're looking at simple rankings. Vincent sees that Job E is clearly dominated by Job B: it's worse on four objectives and equivalent on two. Comparing Job A and Job D, he sees that Job A is better on three objectives, tied on two, and worse on one (vacation). When an alternative has only one advantage over another, as with Job D, it is a candidate for elimination due to practical dominance. In this case, Vincent easily concludes that the one-day vacation advantage of Job D is far outweighed by its disadvantages

Sahid's Ranking Table

	ALTERNATIVES				
Objectives	Job A	Job B	Job C	Job D	Job E
Monthly Salary	3	1	5	4	2
Flexibility	2 (tie)	4	1	2 (tie)	5
Business Skills Development	4	1	3	5	2
Annual Vacation	2	3 (tie)	5	1	3 (tie)
Benefits	1	2 (tie)	5	4	2 (tie)
Enjoyment	1 (tie)	3 (tie)	3 (tie)	1 (tie)	5

in salary, business-skills development, and benefits. Hence, Job D is practically dominated by Job A and can also be eliminated.

Using a ranking table to eliminate dominated alternatives can save you a lot of effort. Sometimes, in fact, it can lead directly to the final decision. If all your alternatives but one are dominated, the remaining alternative is your best choice.

Making Even Swaps

Although it's possible that you'll be down to a single alternative at this point, it's far more likely that you'll still have a number of alternatives to choose from. Because none of the remaining alternatives are dominated, each will have some advantages and some disadvantages relative to each of the others. The challenge now is to make the right trade-offs between them. The even-swap method offers a way to even out the advantages and disadvantages systematically until you are left with a clear choice. (See "Benjamin Franklin's 'Moral or Prudential Algebra'" at the end of this article.)

What do we mean by even swaps? To explain the concept, we need to state an obvious but fundamental tenet of decision making: If every alternative for a given objective is rated equally—for example, if they all cost the same—you can ignore that objective in making your decision. If all airlines charge the same fare for the New York to San Francisco flight, then cost doesn't matter. Your decision will hinge on only the remaining objectives.

The even-swap method provides a way to adjust the values of different alternatives' consequences in order to render them equivalent and thus irrelevant. As its name implies, an even swap increases the value of an alterna-

tive in terms of one objective while decreasing its value
by an equivalent amount in terms of another objective.
If, for example, American Airlines charged $100 more for
a New York to San Francisco flight than did Continental,
you might swap a $100 reduction in the American fare
for 2,000 fewer American frequent-flyer miles. In other
words, you'd "pay" 2,000 frequent flyer miles for the fare
cut. Now American would score the same as Continental
on the cost objective, so cost would have no bearing in
deciding between them. Whereas the assessment of
dominance enables you to eliminate alternatives, the
even-swap method allows you to eliminate objectives. As
more objectives are eliminated, fewer comparisons need
to be made, and the decision becomes easier.

The even-swap method can be a powerful tool in business decision making. Imagine you're running a Brazilian
cola company and several other companies have
expressed interest in buying franchises to bottle and sell
your product. Your company currently has a 20% share
of its market, and it will earn $20 million in the fiscal
year just ending. You have two key objectives for the
coming year: increasing profits and expanding market
share. You estimate that franchising would reduce your
profits to $10 million due to start-up costs, but it would
increase your share to 26%. If you don't franchise, your
profits would rise to $25 million, but your share would
increase only to 21%. You put this all down in a consequences table.

Which is the smart choice? As the table indicates, the
decision boils down to whether the additional $15 mil-
lion profit from not franchising is worth more or less
than the additional 5% market share you would gain
from franchising. To resolve that question, you can apply
the even-swap method following a straightforward process.

First, determine the change necessary to cancel out an objective. If you could cancel out the $15 million profit advantage gained by not franchising, the decision would depend only on market share.

Second, assess what change in another objective would compensate for the needed change. You must determine what increase in market share would compensate for the profit decrease of $15 million. After a careful analysis of the long-term benefits of increased share, you determine that a 3% increase would make up for the lost $15 million.

Third, make the even swap. In the consequences table, you reduce the profit of the not-franchising alternative by $15 million while increasing its market share by 3%. The restated consequences (a $10 million profit and a 24% market share) are equivalent in value to the original consequences (a $25 million profit and a 21% market share). (See the tables "Charting the Consequences" and "Making the Even Swap.")

Fourth, cancel out the now-irrelevant objective. Now that the profits for the two alternatives are equivalent, profit can be eliminated as a consideration in the decision. It all boils down to market share.

Finally, select the dominant alternative. The new decision is easy. The franchising alternative, better on market share than not franchising, is the obvious choice.

For the cola company, only one even swap revealed the superior alternative. Usually, it takes more—often many more. The beauty of the even-swap approach is that no matter how many alternatives and objectives you're weighing, you can methodically reduce the num-

ber of objectives you need to consider until a clear choice
emerges. The method, in other words, is iterative. You
keep eliminating objectives by making additional even
swaps until one alternative dominates all the others or
until only one objective—one basis of comparison—
remains.

Simplifying a Complex Decision

Now that we've discussed each step of the process, let's
apply the whole thing to a more complex business problem. Alan Miller is a computer scientist who started a
technical consulting practice three years ago. For the
first year, he worked out of his home, but as his business
grew he decided to sign a two-year lease on some space
in the Pierpoint office park. Now that lease is about to

Charting the Consequences

	ALTERNATIVES	
Objectives	Franchising	Not franchising
Profit (in millions of $)	10	25
Market Share (%)	26	21

Making the Even Swap

	ALTERNATIVES	
Objectives	Franchising	Not franchising
~~Profit (in millions of $)~~	~~10~~	~~25~~ 10
Market Share (%)	26	~~21~~ 24

expire. He needs to decide whether to renew it or move to a new location.

After considerable thought about his business and its prospects, Alan defines five overriding objectives that he needs his office to fulfill: a short commute from home, good access to his clients, good office services (clerical assistance, copiers and fax machines, and mail service), sufficient space, and low costs. He surveys more than a dozen locations and, dismissing those that clearly fall short of his needs, he settles on five viable alternatives: Parkway, Lombard, Baranov, Montana, and his current building, the Pierpoint.

He then develops a consequences table, laying out the consequences of each alternative for each objective. He uses a different measurement system for each objective. He describes commuting time as the average time in minutes needed to travel to work during rush hour. To measure access to clients, he determines the percentage of his clients whose business is within an hour's lunchtime drive of the office. He uses a simple three-letter scale to describe the office services provided: "A" means full service, including copy and fax machines, telephone answering, and for-fee secretarial assistance; "B" indicates fax machines and telephone answering only; and "C" means that no services are available. Office size is measured in square feet, and cost is measured by monthly rent. (See "Miller's Consequences Table.")

With so many alternatives to compare, Alan immediately seeks to eliminate some by using dominance or practical dominance. To make that easier, he uses the descriptions in the consequences table to create a ranking table. (See "Miller's Ranking Table.")

Scanning the columns, he quickly sees that the Lombard office dominates the current Pierpoint site, out-

ranking it on four objectives and tying it on the fifth. He
eliminates Pierpoint from further consideration. He also
sees that Montana almost dominates Parkway, falling
behind in cost only. Can he eliminate Parkway, too? He
flips back to his original consequences table and notices
that for the small cost disadvantage of Montana—only

Miller's Consequences Table

	ALTERNATIVES				
Objectives	Parkway	Lombard	Baranov	Montana	Pierpoint
Commute in Minutes	45	25	20	25	30
Customer Access (%)	50	80	70	85	75
Office Services	A	B	C	A	C
Office Size (Square Feet)	800	700	500	950	700
Monthly Cost ($)	1850	1700	1500	1900	1750

Miller's Ranking Table

	ALTERNATIVES				
Objectives	Parkway	Lombard	Baranov	Montana	Pierpoint
Commute	5	2 (tie)	1	2 (tie)	4
Customer Access	5	2	4	1	3
Office Services	1 (tie)	3	4 (tie)	1 (tie)	4 (tie)
Office Size	2	3 (tie)	5	1	3 (tie)
Monthly Cost	4	2	1	5	3

$50 per month—he would gain an additional 150 square feet, a much shorter commute, and much better access to clients. He eliminates Parkway using practical dominance.

Alan has reduced his choice to three alternatives—Lombard, Baranov, and Montana—none of which dominates any other. He redraws his consequences table.

To clarify his choice further, Alan needs to make a series of even swaps. In scanning the table, he sees considerable similarity in the commuting times for the three remaining alternatives. If the Baranov's 20-minute commute were increased to 25 minutes using an even swap, the commuting time of all three alternatives would be equivalent, and that objective could be dropped from further consideration. Alan decides that this 5-minute increase in Baranov's commuting time can be compensated for by an 8% increase in Baranov's client access, from 70% to 78%. He makes the swap, rendering commuting time irrelevant in his deliberations. (See the table "Miller's Even Swaps 1.")

Alan then eliminates the office services objective by

Miller's Even Swaps 1

| | ALTERNATIVES | | |
Objectives	Lombard	Baranov	Montana
~~Commute in Minutes~~	~~25~~	~~20~~ ~~25~~	~~25~~
Customer Access (%)	80	~~70~~ 78	85
Office Services	B	C	A
Office Size (Square Feet)	700	500	950
Monthly Cost ($)	1700	1500	1900

making two even swaps with monthly cost. Using the Lombard service level (B) as a standard, he equates an increase in the level of service from C to B for Baranov with a $200 increase in monthly costs. He also equates a decrease in the level of service from A to B for Montana with a savings of $100 per month.

Each time Alan makes an even swap, he changes the way the alternatives match up. Having eliminated the office services objective, he finds that the Baranov alternative is now dominated by the Lombard alternative and can be eliminated. That move highlights an important process consideration. In making even swaps, you should always seek to create dominance where it didn't exist before, thus enabling you to eliminate an alternative. In your decision process, you will want to keep switching back and forth between examining your columns (alternatives) and your rows (objectives), between assessing dominance and making even swaps. (See the table "Miller's Even Swaps 2.")

With Baranov out of the picture, only the Lombard and Montana alternatives remain. They have equivalent

Miller's Even Swaps 2

| | ALTERNATIVES | | |
Objectives	Lombard	Baranov	Montana
~~Commute in Minutes~~	~~25~~	~~25~~	~~25~~
Customer Access (%)	80	78	85
~~Office Services~~	B	~~C~~ B	~~A~~ B
Office Size (Square Feet)	700	500	950
Monthly Cost ($)	1700	~~1500~~ 1700	~~1900~~ 1800

scores in commuting time and services, leaving only
three objectives to consider. Alan next makes an even
swap between office size and monthly cost. Deciding
that the 700-square-foot Lombard office will be cramped,
he equates Montana's additional 250 square feet with a
substantial cost increase—$250 per month. That swap
cancels the office-size objective, revealing Montana to be
the preferred alternative, with advantages in both the
remaining objectives—cost and access to clients. Montana now dominates Lombard. (See the table "Miller's
Even Swaps 3.")

Alan signs the lease for space at Montana, confident
that he has thought through the decision carefully, considered every alternative and objective, and made the
right choice in the end.

The Art of the Swap

Once you get the hang of it, the mechanical part of the
even-swap method becomes easy, almost a game. Determining the relative value of different consequences—the

---

Miller's Even Swaps 3

	ALTERNATIVES	
Objectives	Lombard	Montana
Commute in Minutes	25	25
Customer Access (%)	80	85
Office Services	B	B
Office Size (Square Feet)	700 950	950
Monthly Cost ($)	1700 1950	1800

essence of any trade-off process—is the hard part. By design, the even-swap approach allows you to concentrate on the value determinations one at a time, giving each careful thought. While there's no easy recipe for deciding how much of one consequence to swap for some amount of another consequence—every swap is unique, requiring subjective judgment—you can help ensure that your trade-offs are sound by keeping the following suggestions in mind as you go through the process.

Make the easier swaps first. Determining the value of some consequences will be more difficult than determining the value of others. In choosing among airlines, for example, you may be able to calculate, in fairly precise terms, the monetary value of frequent flyer miles. After all, you know how many miles it would take to earn a free flight. Swapping fares and miles will therefore be a straightforward process. Swapping safety records and flight departure times, however, will be much less clearcut. In that case, you should make the swap between fares and miles—the easier swap—first. Often you will be able to reach a decision (or at least eliminate some alternatives) just by making the easy swaps, and you won't have to wrestle with the hard ones at all.

Concentrate on the amount of the swap, not on the apparent importance of the overall objective. It doesn't make sense to say that one objective is more important than another without considering the actual degree of variation among the consequences of the alternatives under consideration. Is salary more important than vacation? It depends. If the salaries of all the jobs are similar but their vacation times vary widely, the vaca-

tion objective may be more important than the salary
objective.

Concentrating on an objective's overall importance
can get in the way of making wise trade-offs. Consider
the debate that might go on in a town trying to decide
whether public library hours should be cut to save
money. The library advocate declares, "Preserving current library hours is much more important than cutting
costs!" The fiscal watchdog counters, "No, we absolutely
have to cut our budget deficit! Saving money is more
important." If the two sides focused on the actual
amounts of time and money in question, they might find
it easy to reach an agreement. If cutting two hours one
morning a week saves $250,000 annually, the library
advocate might agree that the harm to the library would
be small compared with the amount saved, especially
considering other possible uses for the money. If, instead,
the savings were a mere $25,000 annually, even the fiscal
watchdog might agree that the harm to the library
wouldn't be worth the savings. The point is this: when
you make even swaps, concentrate not on the importance of the objectives but on the importance of the
amounts in question.

**Remember that the value of an incremental change
depends on what you start with.** When you swap a
piece of a larger whole—for example, a portion of an
office's square footage—you need to think of its value in
terms of the whole. For example, adding 300 square feet
to a 700-square-foot office may make the difference
between being cramped and being comfortable, whereas
adding 300 square feet to a spacious 1,000-square-foot
office may not be nearly as valuable to you. The value of

the 300 square feet, like the value of anything being swapped, is relative to what you start with. It's not enough to look only at the size of the slice; you also need to look at the size of the pie.

Make consistent swaps. Although the value of what you swap will be relative, the swaps themselves should be logically consistent. If you would swap A for B and B for C, you should be willing to swap A for C. Let's say you're leading an environmental protection program charged with preserving the wilderness and expanding salmon-spawning habitats for as low a cost as possible. In a cost-benefit analysis, you might calculate that one square mile of wilderness and two miles of spawning habitat along a river both have values equivalent to $400,000. In making your swaps, you should therefore equate one square mile of wilderness with two miles of the river. From time to time, check your swaps for consistency.

Seek out solid information. Swaps between consequences require subjective judgments, but those judgments can be buttressed by solid information and analysis. In making trade-offs involving spawning habitat, for example, you might ask a fish biologist to provide information about how many salmon would use a mile of newly created habitat, how many eggs might eventually hatch, how many fish would survive to swim downstream, and how many would return to spawn in the river years later. Whether a mile of new spawning habitat would result in an increase in the annual salmon run of 20 or 2,000 adult salmon will likely make a big difference in the value you assign to that habitat.

For some decisions, you yourself will be the source of much of the relevant information. If you are trading off vacation time and salary in choosing among job offers,

The process helps you zero in on the real sources of value to your company.

for example, only you can know how you would spend 10 days versus 20 days of vacation and the value of that difference to you. You should be as rigorous in thinking through your own subjective inputs as you are in assessing objective data from outside sources. No matter how subjective a trade-off, you never want to be guided by whim—you must think carefully about the value of each consequence to you.

Our final and perhaps most important bit of advice is an old adage: Practice makes perfect. Like any new approach to an old problem, the even-swap method will take some getting used to. The first few times you make swaps, you may struggle with the overall process as well as with each assessment of value. Fortunately, the process itself is relatively simple, and it always works the same way. Once you get the hang of it, you'll never have to think about it again. Deciding on appropriate swaps, however, will never be easy—each swap will require careful judgment. As you gain experience, though, you'll also gain understanding. You'll become more and more skilled at zeroing in on the real sources of value to you and your company. You'll know what's important and what's not. Perhaps the greatest benefit of the even-swap method is that it forces you to think through the value of every trade-off in a rational, measured way. In the end, that's the secret of making smart choices.

Benjamin Franklin's "Moral or Prudential Algebra"

PEOPLE HAVE ALWAYS STRUGGLED with the difficulties of making trade-offs. More than 200 years ago, Ben Franklin outlined his approach to the challenge in a letter to the noted scientist Joseph Priestly, who was trying to choose between two alternatives.

London
Sept. 19, 1772

Dear Sir,

In the affair of so much importance to you, wherein you ask my advice, I cannot, for want of sufficient premises, advise you *what* to determine, but if you please I will tell you *how*.

When those difficult cases occur, they are difficult, chiefly because while we have them under consideration, all the reasons pro and con are not present to the mind at the same time; but sometimes one set present themselves, and at other times another, the first being out of sight. Hence the various purposes or inclinations alternatively prevail, and the uncertainty that perplexes us.

To get over this, my way is to divide half a sheet of paper by a line into two columns; writing over the one *Pro*, and over the other *Con*. Then, during three or four days consideration, I put down under the different heads short hints of the different motives, that at different times occur to me, *for* or *against* the measure.

When I have thus got them all together in one view, I endeavor to estimate their respective weights; and where I find two, one on each side, that seem equal, I strike them both out. If I find a reason *pro* equal to two reasons *con*, I strike out the three. If I judge some two reasons *con*, equal to some three reasons *pro*, I strike out the five; and thus proceeding I find at length where the balance lies; and if, after a day or two of further consideration, nothing new that is of importance occurs on either side, I come to a determination accordingly.

And, though the weight of reasons cannot be taken with the precision of algebraic quantities, yet, when each is thus considered, separately and comparatively, and the whole lies before me, I think I can judge better, and am less liable to make a rash step; and in fact I have found great advantage from this kind of equation, in what may be called *moral or prudential algebra*.

Wishing sincerely that you may determine for the best, I am ever, my dear friend, yours most affectionately,

B. Franklin

Franklin proposed a wonderful way of using trade-offs to simplify complexity. Each time he eliminated an item from his list of pros and cons, he replaced his original problem with an equivalent but simpler one, ultimately arriving at a clear choice.

Franklin's approach assumes that equivalences—balanced pros and cons—will exist, when in fact they may not. The even-swap approach, by requiring the decision maker to list his or her objectives explicitly and by providing a mechanism for creating equivalence among them, overcomes that flaw. As a result, the approach is applicable to all decisions, not just a few.

Originally published in March–April 1998
Reprint 98206

Humble Decision Making

AMITAI ETZIONI

Executive Summary

OLD-FASHIONED DECISION MAKING doesn't meet the
needs of a world with too much information and too little
time. So-called rational decision making, once the ideal,
requires comprehensive knowledge of every facet of a
problem, which is clearly impossible today. One of the
most recent decision-making models, incrementalism,
despairs of knowledge and instead concentrates on the
smallest possible units of change—without any sense of
grand design.

Now a new model is evolving. It lets us proceed with
partial information. It helps us adapt to new information
as it becomes available. It also helps us achieve broad
goals and purposes. This new model is actually an old
model, used by doctors for centuries and by many managers. It's called mixed scanning or adaptive (or humble)
decision making, and it involves two sets of judgments:

broad, basic choices about an organization's goals and
policies and small, experimental decisions based on in-
depth examination of a focused subset of facts and
choices.

Physicians never commit all their resources and prestige to their first diagnosis. Knowing where they want to
go, they use focused trial and error to get there: try
medicine x for y number of days, and if that doesn't
work, try medicine z. Managers can use this technique to
increase the flexibility and adaptability of their decisions.
In addition, they can put decisions off, stagger them, or
break them into separate parts, and they can also maintain strategic reserves that will allow them to take advantage of sudden opportunities and to cover unexpected
costs.

D ECISION MAKING IN THE 1990s will be even more
of an art and less of a science than it is today. Not only
is the world growing more complex and uncertain at a
faster and faster pace, but the old decision-making
models are failing, and we can expect their failure to
accelerate as well.

If executives once imagined they could gather enough
information to read the business environment like an
open book, they have had to dim their hopes. The flow of
information has swollen to such a flood that managers
are in danger of drowning; extracting relevant data from
the torrent is increasingly a daunting task. Little wonder
that some beleaguered decision makers—even outside
the White House—turn to astrologers and mediums.

Yet from this swelling confusion, a new decision-
making model is evolving, one more attuned to a world

that resembles not so much an open book as an entire
library of encyclopedias under perpetual revision. This
new approach—in fact a very old approach in modern
dress—understands that executives must often proceed
with only partial information, which, moreover, they
have had no time to fully process or analyze. I call this
model "humble decision making."

In a simpler age, the principle governing business
decisions was held to be rationalism. Rationalists argued
that decision makers should and *could* explore every
route that might lead to their goal, collect information
about the costs and utility of each, systematically compare these various alternatives, and choose the most
effective course. Executives were then urged to throw the
full power of their leadership behind the chosen path.
The rule was: Implement! Overcome every adversity! This
called for the kind of assertiveness shown by Israeli army
commanders when they order subordinates to storm and
take a roadblock: "I don't care if you go over it, under it,
around it, or through it, just see that it's ours by the end
of the day."

Today's typical executive finds it quite impossible to
pursue decisions this aggressively. For example, it is no
longer enough to understand the U.S. economy; events in
Brazil, Kuwait, Korea, and a score of other countries are
likely to affect one's decisions. Explosive innovation in
fields like communications, biotechnology, and super-
conductivity can take companies by surprise. Unexpected developments can affect the cost of everything
from raw materials to health care—witness the oil
shocks of the 1970s and the spread of AIDS in the 1980s.
Economic forecasts are proving to be much less reliable
than they used to be (or, perhaps, than we used to think
they were). Deregulation, computer-driven program

trading, foreign hot money in the U.S. economy—all add unpredictability.

Rationalist decision makers simply need to *know* much more than ever before. Of course, with computers our capacity to collect and to semiprocess information has grown, but information is not the same as knowledge. The production of knowledge is analogous to the manufacture of any other product. We begin with the raw material of facts (of which we often have a more than adequate supply). We pretreat these by means of classification, tabulation, summary, and so on, and then proceed to the assembly of correlations and comparisons. But the final product, conclusions, does not simply roll off the production line. Indeed, without powerful overarching explanatory schemes (or theories), whatever knowledge there is in the mountain of data we daily amass is often invisible.

And our prevailing theories—in economics, for instance—are proving ever less suitable to the new age. Artificial intelligence may someday make the mass production of knowledge an easy matter, but certainly not before the year 2000.

In short, the executives of today and tomorrow face continuing information overloads but little growth in the amount of knowledge usable for most complex managerial decisions. Decision makers in the 1990s will continue to travel on unmarked, unlit roads in rain and fog rather than on the broad, familiar, sunlit streets of their own hometowns.

Actually, decision making was never quite as easy as rationalists would have us think. Psychologists argue compellingly that even before our present troubles began, human minds could not handle the complexities that important decisions entailed. Our brains are too limited. At best, we can focus on eight facts at a time. Our ability to calculate probabilities, especially to combine two or more probabilities—essential for most decision making—is low. And the evidence shows that we learn surprisingly slowly. We make the same mistakes over and over again, adjusting our estimates and expectations at an agonizing crawl, and quite poorly at that.

Moreover, we are all prone to let our emotions get in the way—fear, for one. Since all decisions entail risks, decision making almost inevitably evokes anxiety. Decision makers respond in predictable ways that render their decisions less reasonable. Irving L. Janis and Leon Mann have treated this subject at some length in their book, *Decision Making*. Common patterns include defensive avoidance (delaying decisions unduly), overreaction (making decisions impulsively in order to escape the anxious state), and hypervigilance (obsessively collecting more and more information instead of making a decision).

Political factors are another complicating consideration, partly because we try to deny their importance. One study reports that most executives see their decisions as professional, even technocratic, but rarely as political. While they acknowledge that political considerations may enter into dealings with a labor union or a local government and that "bad" political corporations do exist, few are willing to recognize that all corporations are political entities and, consequently, that most if not all important decisions have a political dimension. For example, it is not enough to dream up a new product, market, or research project; we must consider how to build up bases of support among vice presidents, division leaders, and others.

By disregarding the emotions and politics of decision making, rationalism has taught executives to expect more of themselves than is either possible or, indeed, desirable. Implicit in the rationalistic decision model is the assumption that decision makers have unqualified power and wisdom. It ignores the fact that other individuals, too, set goals for themselves and seek to push them through. For ethical reasons, we should not want to override them, and for practical reasons, we cannot do so. Successful decision-making strategies must necessarily include a place for cooperation, coalition building, and the whole panorama of differing personalities, perspectives, responsibilities, and powers.

So even before the world turned ultracomplex and superfungible, our intellectual limitations were such that wholly rational decisions were often beyond our grasp. Recognition of this fact led students of decision making to come up with two new approaches that are, in effect, counsels of despair.

The first of these is called incrementalism, a formal title for what is otherwise known as the science of muddling through. Incrementalism advocates moving not so much toward a goal as away from trouble, trying this or that small maneuver without any grand plan or sense of ultimate purpose. It has two attractive strengths. First, it eliminates the need for complete, encyclopedic information by focusing on limited areas, those nearest to hand, one at a time. And, second, it avoids the danger of grand policy decisions by not making any. Its main weakness is that it is highly "conservative"; it invariably chooses a direction close to the prevailing one. Grand new departures, radical changes in course, do not occur, however much they may be needed.

The second counsel of despair is openly opposed to reflection and analysis. It calls on executives to steam full speed ahead and remake the world rather than seek to understand it. Building on the perfectly accurate observation that many things are exceedingly difficult to predict—which product will sell, what the result of an ad campaign will be, how long R&D will take—executives are advised not to sit back and await sufficient information but to pick the course favored by their experience, inner voice, intuition, and whatever information is readily available—and then to commit. Pumping enough resources, dedication, and ingenuity into the course they have fixed on can make it work, can render an underprocessed decision right.

While more heroic and appealing to the executive self-image than incrementalism, this go-for-it approach is the decision maker's equivalent of "Damn the torpedoes, full speed ahead!" It is a hidden rather than an open counsel of despair, but it does despair of knowing the world and approaching it sensibly. And it is much more likely to end in shipwreck than in victory, especially in ever more treacherous seas.

Yet another approach—rarely described but not as uncommon as it ought to be—is what we might call rational ritualism, where executives and their staffs take part in an information dance whose prescribed moves include the data *pas de deux* and the interpretation waltz, except that the information used is generally poor (arbitrarily selected or from undependable sources) and often vastly overinterpreted. Usually most of those involved (or all of them) know the data is unreliable and the analysis unreal but dare not say that the emperor is naked. Instead, they make ritualistic projections—and know enough to ignore them.

A less explicitly recognized approach to decision making has been with us for centuries. Effective managers have made use of it since business began. Because this approach is particularly well suited to the new age of data overload and pell-mell change, it deserves a new look and, though still evolving, the respectability that a clear formulation can give it. I call it humble decision making, but a more descriptive title might be adaptive decision making or mixed scanning, since it entails a mixture of shallow and deep examination of data—generalized consideration of a broad range of facts and choices followed by detailed examination of a focused subset of facts and choices.

Mixed scanning contrasts strongly with two prevailing models of decision making—rationalism and incrementalism. We have already seen that the rationalist model, which requires full scanning of all relevant data and choices, is often impossible to heed. It requires the collection of enormous quantities of facts, the use of analytic capabilities we do not command, and a knowledge of consequences that are far away in time. Many of those who despair of its usefulness tend to favor incrementalism, or muddling through.

But incrementalism, too, contains a self-defeating feature. Theoretically, incremental decisions are either tentative or remedial—small steps taken in the "right" direction whenever the present course proves to be wrong. But the moment decision makers evaluate their small steps—which they must do in order to determine whether or not the present course is right—they must refer to broader guidelines. These wider criteria are not formulated incrementally but have all the hallmarks of grand, *a priori* decisions, which incrementalism seeks to avoid. Yet without such guidelines, incrementalism amounts to drifting, to action without direction.

Mixed scanning, as the term suggests, involves two sets of judgments: the first are broad, fundamental choices about the organization's basic policy and direction; the second are incremental decisions that prepare the way for new, basic judgments and that implement and particularize them once they have been made. Thus mixed scanning is much less detailed and demanding than rationalistic decision making, but still broader and more comprehensive than incrementalism—and less likely to be limited to familiar alternatives.

Rationalism is a deeply optimistic approach that assumes we can learn all we need to know; mixed scanning is an adaptive strategy that acknowledges our inability to know more than part of what we would need to make a genuinely rational decision. Incrementalism is profoundly cautious and avoids decisions based on partial knowledge; mixed scanning seeks to make the best possible use of partial knowledge rather than proceed blindly with no knowledge at all.

The oldest formal use of mixed scanning is medical. It is the way doctors make decisions. Unlike incrementalists, physicians know what they want to achieve and which parts of the organism to focus on. Unlike rationalists, they do not commit all their resources on the basis of a preliminary diagnosis, and they do not wait for every conceivable scrap of personal history and scientific data before initiating treatment. Doctors survey the general health of a patient, then zero in on his or her particular complaint. They initiate a tentative treatment, and, if it fails, they try something else.

In fact, this is roughly the way effective managers, too, often make decisions. Business data are rarely unequivocal. Driving in fog and rain has always called for caution as well as a clear sense of destination, and the rules for humble yet effective decision making are much the same for doctors and executives.

Focused trial and error is probably the most widely used procedure for adapting to partial knowledge. It has two parts: knowing where to start the search for an effective intervention, and checking outcomes at intervals to adjust and modify the intervention. This approach differs significantly from what we might call outright trial and error, which assumes no knowledge at all, and from fine-tuning searches, which can occur only when knowledge is high and uncertainty low.

Focused trial and error assumes that there is important information that the executive does not have and must proceed without. It is not a question of understanding the world "correctly," of choosing a logical procedure on the basis of facts, but of feeling one's way to an effective course of action despite the lack of essential chunks of data. It is an adaptive, not a rationalistic, strategy.

Tentativeness—a commitment to revise one's course as necessary—is an essential adaptive rule. Physicians tell their patients to take a medicine for x number of days, to call them at once if the symptoms grow worse rather than better, to return after some set interval for another examination. Such safeguards permit the doctor to adjust the intervention if it proves to be ineffective or counterproductive. A good doctor does not invest prestige and ego in the treatment prescribed. On the contrary, what distinguishes good physicians from poor ones is precisely their sensitivity to changing conditions, their pronounced willingness to change directions on the basis of results, their humility in the face of reality.

Executives often render decisions on matters less well understood than many medical conditions. Hence executives, even more than physicians, are best off when they refuse to commit to an initial diagnosis and so refuse to risk dignity and stature on what is inevitably an uncertain course. By viewing each intervention as tentative or experimental, they declare that they fully expect to revise it.

A year ago, some American bankers may have thought it sounded grand to announce that they would play an important role in the new, post-1992 Europe. Now that the great difficulties of such a course have become more evident, those bankers who announced only that they would try to find a way to work within the European Community seem wiser and more prudent.

Procrastination is another adaptive rule that follows from an understanding of the limits of executive knowledge. Delay permits the collection of fresh evidence, the processing of additional data, the presentation of new options. (It can also give the problem a chance to recede untreated.) Rarely is missing the next board meeting as detrimental as it seems. If one can make a significantly strong case at a later board meeting or rezoning hearing or town meeting, the result will justify the delay.

Decision staggering is one common form of delay. If the Federal Reserve believed the discount rate should rise by 3%, it would still not make the adjustment all at once. By adjusting the rate half a point at a time, the Federal Reserve can see a partial result of its intervention under conditions similar to those in which the rest of the intervention, if necessary, will take place.

Fractionalizing is a second corollary to procrastination. Instead of spreading a single intervention over time, it treats important judgments as a series of subdecisions and may or may not also stagger them in time. For example, a company concerned about future interest rates might raise half its needed equity now by issuing a bond and the other half later by selling an asset. Both staggering and fractionalizing allow the company to relate turning points in the decision process to turning points in the supply of information.

Hedging bets is another good adaptive rule. For instance, the less investors know about a specific company, the wiser it is to spread their investments among several stocks. The less certain they are of the stock market in general, the wiser they are to spread their investments among different instruments and areas—bonds and real estate, for example. Hedging bets will never produce a bonanza to compare with the lucky all-or-nothing, eggs-in-one-basket coup, but it is much more likely to improve long-term yield and security.

Maintaining strategic reserves is another form of hedging bets. The stock market investor with a cash reserve after the crashes of 1929 or 1987 was in an excellent position to capitalize on those disasters. In a predictable, rational world, no company would need idle resources. In fact, large reserves can be a dangerous invitation to an LBO. But in a world where we have learned to expect the unexpected, we need reserves to cover unanticipated costs and to respond to unforeseen opportunities.

Reversible decisions, finally, are a way of avoiding overcommitment when only partial information is available. The simplest response to the energy crisis of the early 1970s, for example, was to turn down the thermostat during the winter and raise it during the summer. It had the additional virtue of being fully reversible in seconds. Conservation measures were more difficult to take back, but were often only moderately expensive, and a subsequent lowering of energy prices did not render them counterproductive, even if it did reduce the return on invested capital. Changing an energy source, on the other hand, was often a complex and expensive reaction to the crisis and costly to reverse. Yet a number of companies did convert from oil to coal in the 1970s and now wish they could recall a decision made on the basis of inadequate information and executive overconfidence.

This list of adaptive techniques illustrates several essential qualities of effective decision making that the textbook models miss: flexibility, caution, and the capacity to proceed with partial knowledge, to name just three. Only fools make rigid decisions and decisions with no sense of overarching purpose, while the most able executives already practice more humble decision making than I could possibly preach. They will, I predict, apply the good sense and versatility of this tested, realistic model ever more widely as the world grows more and more difficult to manage.

Originally published in July–August 1989
Reprint 89406

Interpersonal Barriers to Decision Making

CHRIS ARGYRIS

Executive Summary

A MAJOR STUDY of the behavior of 165 top executives in six companies reveals decision-making weaknesses which all management groups have in some degree.

- The actual behavior of top executives during decision-making meetings often does not jibe with their attitudes and prescriptions about effective executive action.

- The gap that often exists between what executives say and how they behave helps create barriers to openness and trust, to the effective search for alternatives, to innovation, and to flexibility in the organization.

59

- These barriers are more destructive in important decision-making meetings than in routine meetings, and they upset effective managers more than ineffective ones.

- The barriers cannot be broken down simply by intellectual exercises. Rather, executives need feedback concerning their behavior and opportunities to develop self-awareness in action. To this end, certain kinds of questioning are valuable; playing back and analyzing tape recordings of meetings has proved to be a helpful step; and laboratory education programs are valuable.

These are a few of the major findings of a study of executive decision making in six representative companies. The findings have vital implications for management groups everywhere; for while some organizations are less subject to the weaknesses described than are others, *all* groups have them in some degree. In this article I shall discuss the findings in detail and examine the implications for executives up and down the line. (For information on the company sample and research methods used in the study, see "Nature of the Study" at the end of this article.)

Words vs. Actions

According to top management, the effectiveness of decision-making activities depends on the degree of innovation, risk taking, flexibility, and trust in the executive system. (Risk taking is defined here as any act where the executive risks his self-esteem. This could be a moment, for example, when he goes against the group view; when he tells someone, especially the person with the highest power, something negative about his impact on the organization; or when he seeks to put millions of dollars in a new investment.)

Nearly 95% of the executives in our study emphasize that an organization is only as good as its top people. They constantly repeat the importance of their responsibility to help themselves and others to develop their abilities. Almost as often they report that the qualities just mentioned—motivation, risk taking, and so on—are key characteristics of any successful executive system. "People problems" head the list as the most difficult, perplexing, and crucial.

In short, the executives vote overwhelmingly for executive systems where the contributions of each executive can be maximized and where innovation, risk taking, flexibility, and trust reign supreme. Nevertheless, the *behavior* of these same executives tends to create decision-making processes that are *not* very effective. Their behavior can be fitted into two basic patterns:

Pattern A—thoughtful, rational, and mildly competitive. This is the behavior most frequently observed during the decision-making meetings. Executives following this pattern own up to their ideas in a style that emphasizes a serious concern for ideas. As they constantly battle for scarce resources and "sell" their views, their openness to others' ideas is relatively high, not because of a sincere interest in learning about the point of view of others, but so they can engage in a form of "one-upmanship"—that is, gain information about the others' points of view in order to politely discredit them.

Pattern B—competitive first, thoughtful and rational second. In this pattern, conformity to ideas replaces concern for ideas as the strongest norm. Also, antagonism to ideas is higher—in many cases higher than openness to ideas. The relatively high antagonism scores usually indicate, in addition to high competitiveness, a high degree of conflict and pent-up feelings.

"Management Groups with Pattern A and Pattern B Characteristics" summarizes data for four illustrative groups of managers—two groups with Pattern A characteristics and two with Pattern B characteristics.

PRACTICAL CONSEQUENCES

In both patterns executives are rarely observed:

- taking risks or experimenting with new ideas or feelings
- helping others to own up, be open, and take risks
- using a style of behavior that supports the norm of individuality and trust as well as mistrust
- expressing feelings, positive or negative

These results should not be interpreted as implying that the executives do not have feelings. We know from the interviews that many of the executives have strong feelings indeed. However, the overwhelming majority (84%) feel that it is a sign of immaturity to express feelings openly *during decision-making meetings*. Nor should the results be interpreted to mean that the executives do not enjoy risk taking. The data permit us to conclude only that few risk-taking actions were *observed* during the meetings. (Also, we have to keep in mind that the executives were always observed in groups; it may be that their behavior in groups varies significantly from their behavior as individuals.)

Management Groups with Pattern A and Pattern B Characteristics

	PATTERN A						PATTERN B			
Total Number of Units Analyzed*	Group 1 198		Group 2 143		Group 3 201		Group 4 131	
Units Characterized by:	Number	Percent	Number	Percent	Number	Percent	Number	Percent
Owning up to Own Ideas	146	74	105	74	156	78	102	78
Concern for Others' Ideas	122	62	89	62	52	26	56	43
Conformity to Others' Ideas	54	27	38	26	87	43	62	47
Openness to Others' Ideas	46	23	34	24	31	15	25	19
Individuality	4	2	12	8	30	15	8	6
Antagonism to Others' Ideas	18	9	4	3	32	16	5	4
Unwillingness to Help Others Own up to Their Ideas	5	2	3	2	14	7	4	3

*A unit is an instance of a manager speaking on a topic. If during the course of speaking he changes to a new topic, another unit is created.

Before I attempt to give my views about the reasons for the discrepancy between executives' words and actions, I should like to point out that these results are not unique to business organizations. I have obtained similar behavior patterns from leaders in education, research, the ministry, trade unions, and government. Indeed, one of the fascinating questions for me is why so many different people in so many different kinds of organizations tend to manifest similar problems.

Why the Discrepancy?

The more I observe such problems in different organizations possessing different technologies and varying greatly in size, the more I become impressed with the importance of the role played by the values or assumptions top people hold on the nature of effective human relationships and the best ways to run an organization.

BASIC VALUES

In the studies so far I have isolated three basic values that seem to be very important:

1. *The significant human relationships are the ones which have to do with achieving the organization's objective.* My studies of over 265 different types and sizes of meetings indicate that executives almost always tend to focus their behavior on "getting the job done." In literally thousands of units of behavior, almost none are observed where the men spend some time in analyzing and maintaining their group's effectiveness. This is true even though in many meet-

ings the group's effectiveness "bogged down" and the objectives were not being reached because of interpersonal factors. When the executives are interviewed and asked why they did not spend some time in examining the group operations or processes, they reply that they were there to get a job done. They add: "If the group isn't effective, it is up to the leader to get it back on the track by directing it."

2. *Cognitive rationality is to be emphasized; feelings and emotions are to be played down.* This value influences executives to see cognitive, intellectual discussions as "relevant," "good," "work," and so on. Emotional and interpersonal discussions tend to be viewed as "irrelevant," "immature," "not work," and so on.

   As a result, when emotions and interpersonal variables become blocks to group effectiveness, all the executives report feeling that they should *not* deal with them. For example, in the event of an emotional disagreement, they would tell the members to "get back to facts" or "keep personalities out of this."

3. *Human relationships are most effectively influenced through unilateral direction, coercion, and control, as well as by rewards and penalties that sanction all three values.* This third value of direction and control is implicit in the chain of command and also in the elaborate managerial controls that have been developed within organizations.

INFLUENCE ON OPERATIONS

The impact of these values can be considerable. For example, to the extent that individuals dedicate themselves to the value of intellectual rationality and "getting the job done," they will tend to be aware of and emphasize the intellectual aspects of issues in an organization and (consciously or unconsciously) to suppress the interpersonal and emotional aspects, especially those which do not seem relevant to achieving the task.

As the interpersonal and emotional aspects of behavior become suppressed, organizational norms that coerce individuals to hide their feelings or to disguise them and bring them up as technical, intellectual problems will tend to arise.

Under these conditions the individual may tend to find it very difficult to develop competence in dealing with feelings and interpersonal relationships. Also, in a world where the expression of feelings is not valued, individuals may build personal and organizational defenses to help them suppress their own feelings or inhibit others in such expression. Or they may refuse to consider ideas which, if explored, could expose suppressed feelings.

Such a defensive reaction in an organization could eventually inhibit creativity and innovation during decision making. The participants might learn to limit themselves to those ideas and values that were not threatening. They might also decrease their openness to new ideas and values. And as the degree of openness decreased, the capacity to experiment would also decrease, and fear of taking risks would increase. This would reduce the *probability* of experimentation, thus decreasing openness to new ideas still further and constricting risk taking even more than formerly. We would thereby have a closed circuit which could become an important cause of loss of vitality in an organization.

Some Consequences

Aside from the impact of values on vitality, what are
some other consequences of the executive behavior patterns earlier described on top management decision
making and on the effective functioning of the organization? For the sake of brevity, I shall include only examples of those consequences that were found to exist in
one form or another in all organizations studied.

RESTRICTED COMMITMENT

One of the most frequent findings is that in major decisions that are introduced by the president, there tends to
be less than open discussion of the issues, and the commitment of the officers tends to be less than complete
(although they may assure the president to the contrary).
For instance, consider what happened in one organization where a major administrative decision made during
the period of the research was the establishment of several top management committees to explore basic long-
range problems:

As is customary with major decisions, the president
discussed it in advance at a meeting of the executive
committee. He began the meeting by circulating, as a
basis for discussion, a draft of the announcement of the
committees. Most of the members' discussion was concerned with raising questions about the wording of the
proposal:

- "Is the word *action* too strong?"

- "I recommend that we change 'steps can be taken' to
'recommendations can be made.'"

- "We'd better change the word 'lead' to 'maintain.' "

As the discussion seemed to come to an end, one executive said he was worried that the announcement of the committees might be interpreted by the people below as an implication "that the executive committee believes the organization is in trouble. Let's get the idea in that all is well."

There was spontaneous agreement by all executives: "Hear, hear!"

A brief silence was broken by another executive who apparently was not satisfied with the concept of the committees. He raised a series of questions. The manner in which it was done was interesting. As he raised each issue, he kept assuring the president and the group that he was not against the concept. He just wanted to be certain that the executive committee was clear on what it was doing. For example, he assured them:

- "I'm not clear. Just asking."

- "I'm trying to get a better picture."

- "I'm just trying to get clarification."

- "Just so that we understand what the words mean."

The president nodded in agreement, but he seemed to become slightly impatient. He remarked that many of these problems would not arise if the members of these new committees took an overall company point of view. An executive commented (laughingly), "Oh, I'm for motherhood too!"

The proposal was tabled in order for the written statement to be revised and discussed further during the next meeting. It appeared that the proposal was the president's personal "baby," and the executive committee members would naturally go along with it. The most responsibility some felt was that they should raise questions so the president would be clear about *his* (not *their*) decision.

At the next meeting the decision-making process was the same as at the first. The president circulated copies of the revised proposal. During this session a smaller number of executives asked questions. Two pushed (with appropriate care) the notion that the duties of one of the committees were defined too broadly.

The president began to defend his proposal by citing an extremely long list of examples, indicating that in his mind "reasonable" people should find the duties clear. This comment and the long list of examples may have communicated to others a feeling that the president was becoming impatient. When he finished, there was a lengthy silence. The president then turned to one of the executives and asked directly, "Why are you worried about this?" The executive explained, then quickly added that as far as he could see the differences were not major ones and his point of view could be integrated with the president's by "changing some words."

The president agreed to the changes, looked up, and asked, "I take it now there is common agreement?" All executives replied "yes" or nodded their heads affirmatively.

As I listened, I had begun to wonder about the commitment of the executive committee members to the idea. In subsequent interviews I asked each about his view of the proposal. Half felt that it was a good proposal. The other half had reservations ranging from moderate to serious. However, being loyal members, they would certainly do their best to make it work, they said.

SUBORDINATE GAMESMANSHIP

I can best illustrate the second consequence by citing from a study of the effectiveness of product planning and program review activities in another of the organizations studied:

It was company policy that peers at any given level should make the decisions. Whenever they could not agree or whenever a decision went beyond their authority, the problem was supposed to be sent to the next higher level. The buck passing stopped at the highest level. A meeting with the president became a great event. Beforehand a group would "dry run" its presentation until all were satisfied that they could present their view effectively.

Few difficulties were observed when the meeting was held to present a recommendation agreed to by all at the lower levels. The difficulties arose when "negative" information had to be fed upward. For example, a major error in the program, a major delay, or a major disagreement among the members was likely to cause such trouble.

The dynamics of these meetings was very interesting. In one case the problem to present was a major delay in a development project. In the dry run the subordinates planned to begin the session with information that "updated" the president. The information was usually presented in such a way that slowly and carefully the president was alerted to the fact that a major problem was about to be announced. One could hear such key phrases as:

- "We are a bit later than expected."

- "We're not on plan."

- "We have had greater difficulties than expected."

- "It is now clear that no one should have promised what we did."

These phrases were usually followed by some reassuring statement such as:

- "However, we're on top of this."

- "Things are really looking better now."

- "Although we are late, we have advanced the state of the art."

- "If you give us another three months, we are certain that we can solve this problem."

To the observer's eyes, it is difficult to see how the president could deny the request. Apparently he felt the same way because he granted it. However, he took nearly 20 minutes to say that this shocked him; he was wondering if everyone was *really* doing everything they could; this was a serious problem; this was not the way he wanted to see things run; he was sure they would agree with him; and he wanted their assurances that this would be the final delay.

A careful listening to the tape after the meeting brought out the fact that no subordinate gave such assurances. They simply kept saying that they were doing their best; they had poured a lot into this; or they had the best technical know-how working on it.

Another interesting observation is that most subordinates in this company, especially in presentations to the president, tended to go along with certain unwritten rules:

1. Before you give any bad news, give good news. Especially emphasize the capacity of the department to work hard and to rebound from a failure.

2. Play down the impact of a failure by emphasizing how close you came to achieving the target or how so on the target can be reached. If neither seems reasonable, emphasize how difficult it is to define such targets, and point out that because the state of the art is so primitive, the original commitment was not a wise one.

3. In a meeting with the president it is unfair to take advantage of another department that is in trouble, even if it is a "natural enemy." The sporting thing to do is say something nice about the other department and offer to help it in any way possible. (The offer is usually not made in concrete form, nor does the department in difficulty respond with the famous phrase, "What do you have in mind?")

The subordinates also were in agreement that too much time was spent in long presentations in order to make the president happy. The president, however, confided to the researcher that he did not enjoy listening to long and, at times, dry presentations (especially when he had seen most of the key data anyway). However, he felt that it was important to go through this because it might give the subordinates a greater sense of commitment to the problem!

LACK OF AWARENESS

One of our most common observations in company studies is that executives lack awareness of their own behavioral patterns as well as of the negative impact of their behavior on others. This is not to imply that they are completely unaware; each individual usually senses some aspects of a problem. However, we rarely find an individual or group of individuals who is aware of enough of the scope and depth of a problem so that the need for effective action can be fully understood.

For example, during the study of the decision-making processes of the president and the 9 vice presidents of a firm with nearly 3,000 employees, I concluded that the members unknowingly behaved in such a way as *not* to encourage risk taking, openness, expression of feelings, and cohesive, trusting relationships. But subsequent interviews with the 10 top executives showed that they held a completely different point of view from mine. They admitted that negative feelings were not expressed, but said the reason was that "we trust each other and respect each other." According to 6 of the men, individuality was high and conformity low; where conformity was agreed to be high, the reason given was the necessity of agreeing with the man who is boss. According to 8 of the men, "We help each other all the time." Issues loaded with conflict were not handled during meetings, it was reported, for these reasons:

- "We should not discuss emotional disagreements before the executive committee because when people are emotional, they are not rational."

- "We should not air our dirty linen in front of the people who may come in to make a presentation."

- "Why take up people's time with subjective debates?"

- "Most members are not acquainted with all the details. Under our system the person who presents the issues has really thought them through."

- "Pre-discussion of issues helps to prevent anyone from sandbagging the executive committee."

- "Rarely emotional; when it does happen, you can pardon it."

The executive committee climate or emotional tone was characterized by such words as:

- "Friendly."

- "Not critical of each other."

- "Not tense."

- "Frank and no tensions because we've known each other for years."

How was I to fit the executives' views with mine? I went back and listened to all the interviews again. As I analyzed the tapes, I began to realize that an interesting set of contradictions arose during many of the interviews. In the early stages of the interviews the executives tended to say things that they contradicted later; "Contradictory Statements" contains examples of contradictions repeated by 6 or more of the 10 top executives.

What accounts for these contradictions? My explanation is that over time the executives had come to mirror, in their behavior, the values of their culture (e.g., be rational, nonemotional, diplomatically open, and so on). They had created a culture that reinforced their own leadership styles. If an executive wanted to behave differently, he probably ran the risk of being considered a deviant. In most of the cases the executives decided to forgo this risk, and they behaved like the majority. These men, in order to live with themselves, probably had to develop various defenses and blinders about their acquiescence to an executive culture that may not have been the one they personally preferred and valued.

Contradictory Statements

During One Part of the Interview an Executive Said:	Yet Later in the Same Interview He Said:
The relationship among executive committee members is "close," "friendly," and based on years of working together.	I do not know how [my peers] feel about me. That's a tough question to answer.
The strength of this company lies in its top people. They are a dedicted, friendly group. We never have the kinds of disagreements and fights that I hear others do.	Yes, the more I think of it, the more I feel this is a major weakness of the company. Management is afraid to hold someone accountable, to say, "You said you would do it. What happened?"
I have an open relationship with my superior.	I have no direct idea how my superior evaluates my work and feels about me.
The group discussions are warm, friendly, not critical.	We trust each other not to upset one another.
We say pretty much what we think.	We are careful not to say anything that will antagonize anyone.
We respect and have faith in each other.	People do not knowingly upset each other, so they are careful in what they say.
The executive committee tackles all issues.	The executive committee tends to spend too much time talking about relatively unimportant issues.
The executive committee makes decisions quickly and effectively.	A big problem of the executive committee is that it takes forever and a day to make important decisions.
The members trust each other.	The members are careful not to say something that may make another member look bad. It may be misinterpreted.
The executive committee makes the major policy decisions.	On many major isues, decisions are really made outside the executive committee meetings. The executive committee convenes to approve a decision and have "holy water" placed on it.

Incidentally, in this group there were two men who had decided to take the other route. Both men were viewed by the others as "a bit rough at the edges" or "a little too aggressive."

To check the validity of some of the findings reported, we interviewed the top 25 executives below the executive committee. If our analysis was correct, we knew, then they should tend to report that the members of the executive committee were low in openness to uncomfortable information, risk taking, trust, and capacity to deal with conflicts openly, and high in conformity. The results were as predicted (see "How the Executive Committee Was Rated by 25 Executives Below It").

BLIND SPOTS

Another result found in all organizations studied is the tendency for executives to be unaware of the negative

How the Executive Committee Was Rated by 25 Executives Below It

Characteristic Rated	NUMBER OF MANAGERS RATING THE COMMITTEE AS:		
	Low	Moderate	High
Openness to Uncomfortable Information*	12	6	4
Risk Taking	20	4	1
Trust	14	9	2
Conformity	0	2	23
Ability to Deal with Conflicts	19	6	0

*Three executives gave a "don't know" response.

feelings that their subordinates have about them. This finding is not startling in view of the fact that the executive problem-solving processes do not tend to reward the upward communication of information about interpersonal issues that is emotionally laden and risky to communicate. To illustrate:

In one organization, all but one of the top executive committee members reported that their relationships with their subordinates were "relatively good to excellent." When asked how they judged their relationships, most of the executives responded with such statements as: "They do everything that I ask for willingly," and "We talk together frequently and openly."

The picture from the middle management men who were the immediate subordinates was different. Apparently, top management was unaware that:

- 71% of the middle managers did not know where they stood with their superiors; they considered their relationships as ambiguous, and they were not aware of such important facts as how they were being evaluated.

- 65% of the middle managers did not know what qualities led to success in their organizations.

- 87% felt that conflicts were very seldom coped with; and that when they were, the attempts tended to be inadequate.

- 65% thought that the most important unsolved problem of the organization was that the top management was unable to help them overcome the intergroup rivalries, lack of cooperation, and poor communications; 53% said that if they could alter one aspect of their superior's behavior, it would be to help him see the "dog eat dog" communication problems that existed in middle management.

- 59% evaluated top management effectiveness as not too good or about average; and 62% reported that the development of a cohesive management team was the second most important unsolved problem.

- 82% of the middle managers wished that the status of their function and job could be increased but doubted if they could communicate this openly to the top management.

Interestingly, in all the cases that I have observed where the president asked for a discussion of any problems that the top and middle management men present thought important, the problems mentioned above were never raised.

Rather, the most frequently mentioned problem (74% of the cases) was the overload problem. The executives and managers reported that they were overloaded and that the situation was getting worse. The president's usual reply was that he appreciated their predicament, but "that is life." The few times he asked if the men had any suggestions, he received such replies as "more help," "fewer meetings," "fewer reports," "delay of schedules," and so on. As we will see, few of these suggestions made sense, since the men were asking either for increases in costs or for a decrease in the very controls that the top management used to administer the organization.

DISTRUST & ANTAGONISM

Another result of the behavior patterns earlier described is that management tends to keep promotions semi-secret and most of the actual reasons for executive changes completely secret. Here is an example from an organization whose board we studied in some detail over a period of two years:

The executives complained of three practices of the board about which the board members were apparently unaware: (1) the constant alteration of organizational positions and charts, and keeping the most up-to-date versions semiconfidential; (2) shifting top executives without adequate discussion with all executives involved and without clearly communicating the real reasons for the move; and (3) developing new departments with product goals that overlapped and competed with the goals of already existing departments.

The board members admitted these practices but tended not to see them as being incompatible with the interests of the organization. For example, to take the first complaint, they defended their practice with such statements as: "If you tell them everything, all they do is worry, and we get a flood of rumors"; "The changes do not *really* affect them"; and, "It will only cut in on their busy schedule and interrupt their productivity."

The void of clear-cut information from the board was, however, filled in by the executives. Their explanations ranged from such statements as "They must be changing things because they are not happy with the way things are going" to "The unhappiness is so strong they do not tell us." Even the executives who profited from some of these moves reported some concern and bewilderment. For example, three reported instances where they had been promoted over some "old-timers." In all cases they were told to "soft-pedal the promotion aspect" until the old-timers were diplomatically informed. Unfortunately, it took months to inform the latter men, and in some cases it was never done.

There was another practice of the board that produced difficulties in the organization:

Department heads cited the board's increasing intervention into the detailed administration of a department when its profit picture looked shaky. This practice was, from these subordinates' view, in violation of the stated philosophy of decentralization.

When asked, board members tended to explain this practice by saying that it was done only when they had doubts about the department head's competence, and then it was always in the interests of efficiency. When they were alerted about a department that was not doing well, they believed that the best reaction was to tighten controls, "take a closer and more frequent look," and "make sure the department head is on top of things." They quickly added that they did not tell the man in question they were beginning to doubt his competence for fear of upsetting him. Thus, again we see how the values of de-emphasizing the expression of negative feelings and the emphasizing of controls influenced the board's behavior.

The department heads, on the other hand, reported different reactions. "Why are they bothered with details? Don't they trust me? If not, why don't they say so?" Such reactions tended to produce more conformity, antagonism, mistrust, and fear of experimenting.

Still another board practice was the "diplomatic" rejection of an executive's idea that was, in the eyes of the board, offbeat, a bit too wild, or not in keeping with the corporate mission. The reasons given by the board for not being open about the evaluation again reflected adherence to the pyramidal values. For example, a board member would say, "We do not want to embarrass them," or "If you really tell them, you might restrict creativity."

This practice tended to have precisely the impact that the superiors wished to *avoid*. The subordinates reacted by asking, "Why don't they give me an opportunity to really explain it?" or "What do they mean when they suggest that the 'timing is not right' or 'funds are not currently available'?"

PROCESSES DAMAGED

It is significant that defensive activities like those described are rarely observed during group meetings dealing with minor or relatively routine decisions. These activities become most noticeable when the decision is an important one in terms of dollars or in terms of the impact on the various departments in the organization. *The forces toward ineffectiveness operate most strongly during the important decision-making meetings.* The group and organizational defenses operate most frequently when they can do the most harm to decision-making effectiveness.

Another interesting finding is that the more effective and more committed executives tend to be upset about these facts, whereas the less effective, less committed people tend simply to lament them. They also tend to take on an "I told them so" attitude—one of resignation and noninvolvement in correcting the situation. In short, it is the better executives who are negatively affected.

What Can Be Done?

What can the executive do to change this situation?

I wish that I could answer this question as fully as I should like to. Unfortunately, I cannot. Nevertheless, there are some suggestions I can make.

BLIND ALLEYS

First, let me state what I believe will *not* work.

Learning about these problems by listening to lectures, reading about them, or exploring them through cases is not adequate; an article or book can pose some issues and get thinking started, but—in this area, at least—it cannot change behavior. Thus, in one study with 60 top executives:

Lectures were given and cases discussed on this subject for nearly a week. A test at the end of the week showed that the executives rated the lecturers very high, liked the cases, and accepted the diagnoses. Yet when they attempted to apply their new-found knowledge outside the learning situation, most were unable to do so. The major problem was that they had not learned how to make these new ideas come to life in their behavior.

As one executive stated, pointing to his head: "I know up here what I should do, but when it comes to a real meeting, I behave in the same old way. It sure is frustrating."[2]

Learning about these problems through a detailed diagnosis of executives' behavior is also not enough. For example:

I studied a top management group for nearly four months through interviews and tape recordings of their decision-making meetings. Eventually, I fed back the analysis. The executives agreed with the diagnosis as well as with the statement by one executive that he found it depressing. Another executive, however, said he now felt that he had a clearer and more coherent picture of some of the causes of their problems, and he was going to change his behavior. I predicted that he would probably find that he would be unable to change his behavior—

and even if he did change, his subordinates, peers, and superiors might resist dealing with him in the new way.

The executive asked, "How can you be so sure that we can't change?" I responded that I knew of no case where managers were able to alter successfully their behavior, their group dynamics, and so forth by simply realizing intellectually that such a change was necessary. The key to success was for them to be able to show these new strategies in their behavior. To my knowledge, behavior of this type, groups with these dynamics, and organizational cultures endowed with these characteristics were very difficult to change. What kind of thin-skinned individuals would they be, how brittle would their groups and their organizations be if they could be altered that easily?

Three of the executives decided that they were going to prove the prediction to be incorrect. They took my report and studied it carefully. In one case the executive asked his subordinates to do the same. Then they tried to alter their behavior. According to their own accounts, they were unable to do so. The only changes they reported were (1) a softening of the selling activities, (2) a reduction of their aggressive persuasion, and (3) a genuine increase in their asking for the subordinates' views.

My subsequent observations and interviews uncovered the fact that the first two changes were mistrusted by the subordinates, who had by now adapted to the old behavior of their superiors. They tended to play it carefully and to be guarded. This hesitation aggravated the executives, who felt that their subordinates were not responding to their new behavior with the enthusiasm that they (the superiors) had expected.

However, *the executives did not deal with this issue openly*. They kept working at trying to be rational, patient, and rewarding. The more irritated they became and the more they showed this irritation in their behavior, the more the subordinates felt that the superiors' "new" behavior was a gimmick.

Eventually, the process of influencing subordinates slowed down so much that the senior men returned to their more controlling styles. The irony was that in most cases the top executives interpreted the subordinates' behavior as proof that they needed to be needled and pushed, while the subordinates interpreted the top managers' behavior as proof that they did not trust their assistants and would never change.

The reason I doubt that these approaches will provide anything but temporary cures is that they do not go far enough. If changes are going to be made in the behavior of an executive, if trust is to be developed, if risk taking is to flourish, he must be placed in a different situation. He should be helped to (a) expose his leadership style so that he and others can take a look at its true impact; (b) deepen his awareness of himself and the dynamics of effective leadership; and (c) strive for these goals under conditions where he is in control of the amount, pace, and depth of learning.

These conditions for learning are difficult to achieve. Ideally, they require the help of a professional consultant. Also, it would be important to get away from the organization—its interruptions, pressures, and daily administrative tensions.

VALUE OF QUESTIONS

The executive can strive to be aware that he is probably programmed with a set of values which cause him to behave in ways that are not always helpful to others and which his subordinates will not discuss frankly even when they believe he is not being helpful. He can also strive to find time to uncover, through careful questioning, his impact on others. Once in a while a session that is focused on the "How am I doing?" question can enlighten the executive and make his colleagues more flexible in dealing with him.

One simple question I have heard several presidents ask their vice presidents with success is: "Tell me what, if anything, I do that tends to prevent (or help) your being the kind of vice president you wish to be?" These presidents are careful to ask these questions during a time when they seem natural (e.g., performance review sessions), or they work hard ahead of time to create a climate so that such a discussion will not take the subordinate by surprise.

Some presidents feel uncomfortable in raising these questions, and others point out that the vice presidents are also uncomfortable. I can see how both would have such feelings. A chief executive officer may feel that he is showing weakness by asking his subordinates about his impact. The subordinate may or may not feel this way, but he may sense that his chief does, and that is enough to make him uncomfortable.

Yet in two companies I have studied where such questions were asked, superiors and subordinates soon learned that authority which gained strength by a lack of openness was weak and brittle, whereas authority resting on open feedback from below was truly strong and viable.

WORKING WITH THE GROUP

Another step that an executive can take is to vow not to accept group ineffectiveness as part of life. Often I have heard people say, "Groups are no damned good; strong leadership is what is necessary." I agree that many groups are ineffective. I doubt, however, if either of the two leadership patterns described earlier will help the situation. As we have seen, both patterns tend to make the executive group increasingly less effective.

If my data are valid, the search process in executive decision making has become so complicated that group participation is essential. No one man seems to be able to have all the knowledge necessary to make an effective decision. If individual contributions are necessary in group meetings, it is important that a climate be created that does not discourage innovation, risk taking, and honest leveling between managers in their conversations with one another. The value of a group is to maximize individual contributions.

Interestingly, the chief executive officers in these studies are rarely observed making policy decisions in the classic sense, viz., critical selections from several alternatives and determination of future directions to be taken. This does not mean that they shy away from taking responsibility. Quite the contrary. Many report that they enjoy making decisions by themselves. Their big frustration comes from realizing that most of the major decisions they face are extremely complex and require the coordinated, honest inputs of many different executives. They are impatient at the slowness of meetings, the increasingly quantitative nature of the inputs, and, in many cases, their ignorance of what the staff groups did to the decision inputs long before they received them.

The more management deals with complexity by the use of computers and quantitative approaches, the more it will be forced to work with inputs of many different people, and the more important will be the group dynamics of decision-making meetings. If anyone doubts this, let him observe the dry runs subordinates go through to get a presentation ready for the top. He will observe, I believe, that much data are included and excluded by subordinates on the basis of what they believe those at the top can hear.

In short, *one of the main tasks of the chief executive is to build and maintain an effective decision-making network*. I doubt that he has much choice *except* to spend time in exploring how well his group functions.

Such explorations could occur during the regular workday. For example:

In one organization the president began by periodically asking members of his top group, immediately after a decision was made, to think back during the meeting and describe when they felt that the group was not being as effective as they wished. How could these conditions be altered?

As trust and openness increased, the members began to level with each other as to when they were inhibited, irritated, suppressed, confused, and withholding information. The president tried to be as encouraging as he could, and he especially rewarded people who truly leveled. Soon the executives began to think of mechanisms they could build into their group functioning so they would be alerted to these group problems and correct them early. As one man said, "We have not eliminated all our problems, but we are building a competence in our group to deal with them effectively if and when they arise."

UTILIZING FEEDBACK

Another useful exercise is for the superior and his group members to tape-record a decision-making meeting, especially one which is expected to be difficult. At a later date, the group members can gather and listen to the tape. I believe it is safe to say that simply listening to the tape is an education in itself. If one can draw from skilled company or outside help, then useful analyses can be made of group or individual behavior.

Recently, I experimented with this procedure with an "inside" board of directors of a company. The directors met once a month and listened to tape recordings of their monthly board meetings. With my help they analyzed their behavior, trying to find how they could improve their individual and group effectiveness. Listening to tapes became a very involving experience for them. They spent nearly four hours in the first meeting discussing less than ten minutes of the tape.

'Binds' created.   One of the major gains of these sessions was that the board members became aware of the "binds" they were creating for each other and of the impact they each had on the group's functioning. Thus:

Executive A was frequently heard antagonizing Executive B by saying something that B perceived as "needling." For example, A might seem to be questioning B's competence. "Look here," he would say, "anyone who can do simple arithmetic should realize that. . . ."

Executive B responded by fighting. B's way of fighting back was to utilize his extremely high capacity to verbalize and intellectualize. B's favorite tactic was to show A where he missed five important points and where his logic was faulty.

Executive A became increasingly upset as the "barrage of logic" found its mark. He tended to counteract by (a) remaining silent but manifesting a sense of being flustered and becoming red-faced; and/or (b) insisting that his logic *was* sound even though he did not express it in "highfalutin language" as did B.

Executive B pushed harder (presumably to make A admit he was wrong) by continuing his "barrage of logic" or implying that A could not see his errors because he was upset.

Executive A would respond to this by insisting that he was not upset. "The point you are making is so simple, why, anyone can see it. Why should I be upset?"

Executive B responded by pushing harder and doing more intellectualizing. When Executive A eventually reached his breaking point, he too began to shout and fight.

At this point, Executives C, D, and E could be observed withdrawing until A and B wore each other out.

Progress achieved.   As a result of the meetings, the executives reported in interviews, board members experienced fewer binds, less hostility, less frustration, and more constructive work. One member wondered if the group had lost some of its "zip," but the others disagreed. Here is an excerpt from the transcript of one discussion on this point:

Executive A: My feeling is, as I have said, that we have just opened this thing up, and I for one feel that we have benefited a great deal from it. I think I have improved; maybe I am merely reflecting the fact that you [Executive B] have improved. But at least I think there has been improvement in our relationship. I also see signs of not as good a relationship in other places as there might be.

I think on the whole we are much better off today than we were a year ago. I think there is a whole lot less friction today than there was a year ago, but there's still enough of it.

Now we have a much clearer organization setup; if we were to sit down here and name the people, we would probably all name exactly the same people. I don't think there is much question about who should be included and who should not be included; we've got a pretty clean organization.

Executive B: You're talking now about asking the consultant about going on with this week's session?

Executive A: It would be very nice to have the consultant if he can do it; then we should see how we can do it without him, but it'd be better with him.

Executive B: But that's the step, as I understand it, that should be taken at this stage. Is that right?

Executive A: Well, I would certainly favor doing something; I don't know what. I'm not making a specific recommendation; I just don't like to let go of it.

Executive C: What do you think?

Executive D: I'm not as optimistic as A. I wonder if anybody here agrees with me that maybe we haven't made as much progress as we think. I've personally enjoyed these experiences, and I'd like to see them continued.

Executive A: Would you like to venture to say why I think we have made progress and why I might be fooled?

Executive D: Well, I think maybe you are in the worst position to evaluate progress because if the worst possible thing that can happen is for people to no longer fight and struggle, but to say, "yes, sir," you might call that progress. That might be the worst thing that could happen, and I sort of sense some degree of resignation—I don't think it's progress. I don't know. I might be all alone in this. What do you think?

Executive C: On one level it is progress. Whether it is institutional progress and whether it produces commensurate institutional benefits is a debatable question. It may in fact do so. I think it's very clear that there is in our meetings and in individual contact less heat, less overt friction, petulance, tension, than certainly was consistently the case. Do you agree?

Executive C: Yes, I think so.

Executive D: It has made us a great deal more aware of the extent and nature of the friction and clearly has made all of us intent on fighting less. There's some benefit to it; but there are some drawbacks.

Executive A: Well, if you and D are right, I would say for that reason we need more of the program.

LABORATORY TRAINING

Another possibility is for the executive to attend a program designed to help increase competence in this area, such as laboratory education and its various offshoots ("T-groups," the "managerial grid," "conflict management labs," and so on[3]). These learning experiences are available at various university and National Training Laboratory executive programs. They can also be tailor-made for the individual organization.

I believe outside programs offer the better way of becoming acquainted with this type of learning. Bear in mind, though, that since typically only one or two executives attend from the same organization, the biggest payoff is for the individual. The inside program provides greater possibilities for payoff to the organization.

At the same time, however, it should also be kept in mind that in-house programs *can* be dangerous to the organization. I would recommend that a thorough study be made ahead of time to ascertain whether or not a laboratory educational experience would be helpful to company executives individually and to the organization.

OPEN DISCUSSION

I have never observed a group whose members wanted it to decay. I have never studied a group or an organization that was decaying where there were not some members who were aware that decay was occurring. Accordingly, one key to group and organizational effectiveness is to get this knowledge out into the open and to discuss it thoroughly. The human "motors" of the group and the organization have to be checked periodically, just as does the motor of an automobile. Without proper maintenance, all will fail.

Nature of the Study

THE SIX COMPANIES STUDIED INCLUDE: (1) an electronics firm with 40,000 employees, (2) a manufacturer and marketer of a new innovative product with 4,000 employees, (3) a large research and development company with 3,000 employees, (4) a small research and development organization with 150 employees, (5) a consulting-research firm with 400 employees, and (6) a producer of heavy equipment with 4,000 employees.

The main focus of the investigation reported here was on the behavior of 165 top executives in these companies. The executives were board members, executive committee members, upper-level managers, and (in a few cases) middle-level managers.

Approximately 265 decision-making meetings were studied and nearly 10,000 units of behavior analyzed. The topics of the meetings ranged widely, covering investment decisions, new products, manufacturing problems, marketing strategies, new pricing policies, administrative changes, and personnel issues. An observer took notes during all but 10 of the meetings; for research purposes, these 10 were analyzed "blind" from tapes (i.e., without ever meeting the executives). All other meetings were taped also, but analyzed at a later time.

The major device for analyzing the tapes was a new system of categories for scoring decision-making meetings.[1] Briefly, the executives' behavior was scored according to how often they—

- owned up to and accepted responsibility for their ideas or feelings;
- opened up to receive others' ideas or feelings;
- experimented and took risks with ideas or feelings;
- helped others to own up, be open, and take risks;
- did not own up; were not open; did not take risks; and did not help others in any of these activities.

A second scoring system was developed to produce a quantitative index of the *norms* of the executive culture. There were both positive and negative norms. The positive norms were:

1. *Individuality*, especially rewarding behavior that focused on and valued the uniqueness of each individual's ideas and feelings.
2. *Concern* for others' ideas and feelings.
3. *Trust* in others' ideas and feelings.

The negative norms were:

1. *Conformity* to others' ideas and feelings.

2. *Antagonism* toward these ideas and feelings.

3. *Mistrust* of these ideas and feelings.

In addition to our observations of the men at work, at least one semistructured interview was conducted with each executive. All of these interviews were likewise taped, and the typewritten protocols served as the basis for further analysis.

Since values arise from basic psychological characteristics of man, it is not the existence or nonexistence of values that distinguishes a man from his neighbor. Further, the variety of experience that marks contemporary life makes conflict in values an inescapable adjunct to living.

Where men differ, thus, is the manner in which they meet and resolve this conflict—a conflict that cannot be avoided. Unpleasant problems can be temporarily ignored or denied, and value conflicts are frequently afforded this treatment. Solutions of convenience can be implemented with life departmentalized and fragmented. These are the solutions of men who see most problems as unpleasant.

There are those, however, for whom a problem can be a challenge to understanding. For the man who sees in his values the core of his individuality, the solution of value conflicts becomes a matter of the greatest importance. It is this type of man—and his experience—who suggests the only available answer to the problem of conflicting values.

And the answer is nothing more than the realization that, for the time being, there is no pat answer. It is possible that there will never be a solution other than this. Achievements will always, hopefully, fall short of aspirations. Each new experience brings the possibility of even richer insights. Progress is made, but the farther man proceeds the more rapidly his horizons broaden.

Consequently, the central question for the businessman is not how material and spiritual values can be brought into agreement, but how to live with the inner stress of always falling somewhat short of one's own ideals. The challenge is finding for oneself, through consistent, constructive, and creative effort, those ideals which will lead him on to a more meaningful and purposeful life.

Staff of Rohrer, Hibler & Replogle, Managers for Tomorrow, *edited by Charles D. Flory, General Partner, New York, The New American Library, Inc., 1965, pp. 262-263.*

Notes

1. For a detailed discussion of the system of categories, and other aspects of methodology, see my book, *Organization and Innovation* (Homewood, Illinois, Richard D. Irwin, Inc., 1965).

2. See my article, "Explorations in Interpersonal Competence II," *Applied Behavioral Science,* Vol. 1, No. 3, 1965, p. 255.

3. For detailed discussions of such variations see my article, "T-Groups for Organizational Effectiveness," HBR March–April 1964, p. 60; R. R. Blake, J. S. Mouton, L. B. Barnes, and L. E. Greiner, "Breakthrough in Organization Development," HBR November–December 1964, p. 135; and Edgar Schein and Warren Bennis, Personal and Organizational Change Through Laboratory Methods (New York, John Wiley & Sons, 1965).

Originally published in March–April 1966
Reprint 66201

Can You Analyze
This Problem?

PERRIN STRYKER

Executive Summary

IT POSES DIFFICULT QUESTIONS concerning production, labor relations, and personnel. The manager who is trying to resolve these dilemmas needs your help. (There will be a sequel.)

THE ABILITY OF MANAGERS to solve problems and make decisions rationally has long been assumed to be one of the valuable products of experience on the job. But close observation of their actual practices has shown that even veteran managers are likely to be very unsystematic when dealing with problems and decisions. And their hit-or-miss methods often produce decisions based on erroneous conclusions, which means that the decisions must also be wrong.

Some years ago, the surprisingly inefficient ways in which managers use information led Charles H. Kepner, a social psychologist, and Benjamin B. Tregoe, a sociologist, to develop a systematic approach to problem solving and decision making. A description of the research and training methods developed by Kepner-Tregoe and Associates of Princeton, N.J, was presented to HBR readers in an earlier issue.[1] And by now more than 15,000 experienced managers in major corporations have been trained in their concepts of problem analysis and decision making. These concepts are shortly to be published in book form.[2]

Practically every manager who has taken this training has been rather rudely shocked to discover how faulty his own reasoning methods have been in handling problems and decisions. Readers are therefore invited to test their own reasoning powers against the problems presented in the case history, based directly on an actual situation, set forth below.

The Burred Panels

The problems to be solved are presented in the form of dialogues between various managers in a plant which manufactures quarter panels—the body parts that cover the front quarters of the car, including the wheels. The quarter panel is the successor to the fender, and is the part most often damaged in collisions in traffic accidents. This plant has 3,000 employees and makes not only quarter panels but many other smaller parts and components for two of the models sold by one of the Big Three auto companies.

The panels are made on four separate production lines, each line headed by a huge hydraulic press that stamps the panels out of sheet-steel blanks. When the flat steel arrives at the plant from various suppliers by rail, it is unloaded and carried to a machine which cuts identical-size blanks for all four hydraulic presses. Blanks go to the presses by forklift trucks in pallet stacks of 40 each, and the schedule is so arranged that there is always a supply on hand when the presses are started up on the morning shift.

THE PRINCIPALS

Since this problem, like any other management problem, involves different types of people, the following brief descriptions of the characters, whose names have been disguised, may be useful:

- Oscar Burger, Plant Manager—a tough manager in his late fifties; known for his willingness to listen to others; considered antiunion by the employees.

- Robert Polk, Production Chief—a hard-nosed driver, very able technically, but quick-tongued and inclined to favor certain subordinates; also considered antiunion by the employees.

- Ben Peters, Quality Control Manager—reserved, quiet, and cautious when dealing with others; extremely confident in his figures.

- Ralph Coggin, Industrial Relations Manager—a fairly typical personnel manager; sympathetic to employees; relies on human relations techniques in dealing with the union.

- Andy Patella, Shop Steward—antagonistic to management and eager to prove his power; has developed rapport with Industrial Relations Manager Coggin.

- George Adams, Supervisor on Line #1—steady, solid, and well respected by his men.

- James Farrell, Supervisor on Line #2—irascible, ambitious, and somewhat puritanical; very antiunion.

- Henry Dawson, Supervisor on Line #3—patient, warmhearted, and genuinely liked by his men.

- Otto Henschel, Supervisor on Line #4—aloof, cool, and a bit ponderous; neither liked nor disliked by his men.

MORNING EMERGENCY

The situation opens at 11:00 A.M. on a Wednesday in the office of Plant Manager Oscar Burger, who has called an emergency meeting. Fifty minutes ago he learned from Production Chief Bob Polk that nearly 10% of the panels coming off lines #1 and #2 were being rejected by Quality Control because of burrs and other rough spots.

Burger: I've called you in here because we're in real trouble if we can't lick this reject problem fast. The company needs all the panels we can ship, and more, if it's going to catch up with this new-model market. Both new models of the Panther and the Cheetah are going over big, and if we slow down on panels, the old man in Detroit will be on my neck fast. So let's get all the facts out on the table and run this thing down before lunch. Bob here tells me Line #1 started putting out rejects about three minutes after the end of the 10 o'clock relief break and Line #2 went wild about 9:30. Bob, suppose you tell us just what you've found out so far.

Polk: You've about covered it, Oscar. Farrell, the supervisor now on Line #2, says he's checked several times to see if these burrs in the panels are being caused by something in the sheets, but he hasn't found anything suspicious. Sheets all look nice and clean going into the press, but many come out rough as hell. He says the inspectors report that rejects rose from the normal one or two an hour to eight or nine in the last hour. On Line #1, George Adams says it's about the same story, and he can't figure it out—it just started up suddenly after the relief break.

Burger: Doesn't Farrell or Adams have *any* idea why it started?

Polk: Well, Farrell is sure it's deliberate sabotage by the drawpress operators, but he can't catch them at it. He says it's not hard to produce burrs and rough spots if a man positions a sheet just slightly wrong. He says the men on his line are mad as hell over his suspending Joe Valenti yesterday, and he had another argument when Valenti came in this morning against orders and tried to take back his press job. Farrell called the guard and had Valenti escorted to the gate.

Burger: What's that? I never heard about this. What's wrong with Valenti? *(He turns to Industrial Relations Manager Coggin.)* Ralph, what about this?

Coggin: Oh, I don't think it's all Valenti's fault. He and Farrell have been at it for a long time, as you no doubt know, arguing over management's rights. Farrell says he saw Valenti go behind the tool crib yesterday afternoon during the relief break, and Farrell swears Valenti had a bottle with him. He caught Valenti drinking on the job last year, you remember, and says he wishes he'd fired Valenti then instead of suspending him. You know how Farrell is about liquor, especially on the job. Anyway, he accused Valenti of drinking on the job again, and after some hot words he sent Valenti home for the rest of the week. Andy Patella, the shop steward, protested Farrell's action immediately, of course.

Polk: Farrell's OK, Ralph; he's doing his job.

Burger: Let's get back to this reject problem. What has Valenti got to do with it?

Coggin: Well, I talked with Patella, and he reports the men on all four lines are sore as hell. They made some sharp cracks about Farrell being a union-buster yesterday after the argument and again this morning when he threw Valenti out. When the drawpress on #2 started putting out a lot of rejects on Panther panels, and Quality Control reported this to Farrell, he went over to the press operator and made some suggestions on placing the sheets, or something like that. The man just glared at him and said nothing, Patella tells me, and Farrell finally walked away. The reject rate stayed high, and during the whole 15 minutes of the relief break the men from all the lines were talking together about Valenti's case. Patella says Valenti's young brother, Pete, a spot welder who works on Line #3 under Dawson, called for a walkout, and quite a few seemed to think it was a good idea—contract or no contract. Then right after the men went back to work, Line #1 started to throw off rejects at a high rate.

Burger: What does Adams think about this, Ralph?

Coggin: He won't completely buy that sabotage theory of Farrell's, but he admits there doesn't seem to be any other explanation. The maintenance troubleshooters have been all over the press and can't find anything wrong. The die is OK, and the hydraulic system is OK. They made some adjustments on the iron claw that removes the piece from the press, but that's all.

Burger (turning to Quality Control Manager Ben Peters): Ben, what is your idea about this?

Peters: It's hard to say what might be causing it. We've been checking the sheets from Zenith Metals we started using this morning, and they looked perfect going through the blanker. Besides, it's only on lines #1 and #2 that we're getting burrs, so maybe we've got trouble with those presses.

Polk: I'll check it with Engineering, but I'm willing to bet my last dollar the presses are OK.

Burger: Yes, I think you can forget about trouble in the presses, Ben. And the blanker's never given us a hard time, ever. Still, you'd better have Engineering check that too, Bob, just in case. Meanwhile, I'd like to. . . . *(He pauses while the door opens and Burger's secretary slips in and hands Peters a note.)*

Peters: I'll be damned! My assistant, Jerry, tells me that Line #4 has just begun turning out a mess of burred rejects. I wouldn't have thought that slow old line could go haywire like that—those high-speed presses on the other lines, maybe, but not on Henschel's steady old #4 rocking along at 50 panels an hour.

Polk: Well, that seems to knock out a theory I was getting ready to offer. With #4 acting up, too, it looks like the press speeds aren't to blame. Now I guess we won't have long to wait before Dawson's line also starts bugging up the blanks.

Coggin: Maybe #3 won't go sour if what Patella says about Dawson is true. He says Dawson's men would go all out for him if he asked them, and gather Patella hasn't had much success selling them on his anticompany tactics.

Burger: What's he peddling now?

Coggin: Same old stuff. He claims the company is trying to discredit the union with the men, especially now that contract negotiations are coming up next month. This year he's also tossed in the rumor that the company will threaten to abandon this plant and move out of the state if the union does not accept the local package of benefits management offers in negotiations.

Burger: That's stupid. Hell, when will the union wake up and give us a fair day's work for the pay they're getting? But let's stop this chatter and get after these rejects. Check anything and everything you can think of. We can't afford to shut any line down with the factory as tight as it is on Panther panels. Let's meet back here at 4 o'clock this afternoon.

INFORMAL GET-TOGETHER

The meeting breaks up, and Polk goes to the shop floor to check on the presses and the blanker. Peters goes to his quality-control records to see when the reject rate last hit its current level. Industrial Relations Manager Coggin seeks out Patella to check on Farrell's handling of Valenti and the other men on his line. During the lunch hour in the cafeteria, an informal meeting of the four supervisors and Production Chief Bob Polk takes place.

Farrell: I suppose you got the boss all straightened out on those rejects, Bob. That Valenti has a lot of buddies, and we'll need to keep our eyes peeled to actually catch them fouling up the stampings.

Henschel: You can say that again! I've got a couple of Valenti's old buddies on my line, and ever since the burrs started showing up about 11:20, they've been extra careful. I've traced at least three rejects that I think I can attribute to him.

Polk: Keep a count on who makes the most rejects, and maybe we can pin this down to a few sore-heads.

Adams: You fellas sound like you're on a manhunt. As for me, I think Engineering will come up with the answer. The press on my line has been making more noise than usual today, and I think there's something fishy there. Right now, Bob, I'd like your help in getting the night shift to cut down on the number of stacks of blanks they leave us for the morning runs. It'd help a lot if they'd keep it down to two stacks of 40 each. Again this morning I had four stacks cluttering up my area.

Polk: I'll see what we can do with Scheduling.

Henschel: I'm with you there, Adams. I've been loaded with four stacks for the last five days running. With my slow-speed old equipment, I could manage nicely with only one stack to start off. I noticed that Farrell had two stacks and Dawson had only one to start his line today, and why should they be getting favors?

Dawson: Now, Otto, you're just jealous of my new high-speed press. You got an old clunker, and you know it. What you need is to get off that diet of Panther panels and join me banging out those shallow-draw panels for the Cheetah. Also, it might help you to smile now and then when one of your men cracks a joke. Remember that old proverb, "He that despiseth small things shall fall by little and little."

Farrell: I can think of another proverb that you might consider, Dawson. "Spare the rod and spoil the child." Is it true that your crew is going to win a trip to Bermuda if they're all good boys and make nothing but good panels?

Adams: Aw, cut it, Farrell. We can't all be tough guys.

Farrell: Well anyway, I'm glad Dawson didn't have to cope with Valenti today. That boozer is finally out of my hair. I can't forget last year when he helped Patella spread the word that if the men would burr a lot of the stampings, they could pressure management into a better contract. I wouldn't be surprised if Valenti and Patella were in cahoots now, trying the same angle before negotiations start.

Adams: Relax, Farrell. You can't prove that's so. The men aren't as dumb as all that, as last year proved when they refused to believe Patella. What bugs me is those rejects this morning. Never saw so many bad burrs show up so fast.

Henschel: They sure surprised me, too, but you know I think Quality Control may be a little bit overexcited about the burrs. I figure all of them could be reamed and filed out with a little handwork. Put two extra men on the line, and it would be all taken care of.

Farrell: Maybe so, but you know how Burger would feel about the extra costs on top of the lower output. And don't forget, Henschel, our high-speed presses are banging out 30 more an hour than yours. Well, I gotta get back and see what's with Valenti's buddies on my line.

ASIDE CONVERSATION

All the supervisors get up and leave together. They pay no attention to Industrial Relations Manager Coggin talking with Shop Steward Patella in a corner of the cafeteria.

Coggin: What I want to know, Patella, is why did Valenti try to get back on the line this morning against Farrell's orders?

Patella: Why not? Farrell was miles off base sending Joe home yesterday without telling me or you or anyone else. I was glad Joe came back and faced that s.o.b. Farrell's been getting jumpier and jumpier lately, and do you know what they say? They say he's cracking up over that poor kid of his—the little teenager who's turned out to be such a tramp. I feel sorry for him, but that's no reason why he has to take his feelings out on his men. His crew won't take it much longer, and the other crews are sore, too. You know Valenti's brother this morning over on Line #3 began talking about a walkout?

Coggin: Yes, I heard he did. So why didn't they go out?

Patella: Oh, that crew of Dawson's is too company-minded, and there are some older men there who almost worship Dawson. But they'll go out if management doesn't wise up and respect their rights.

Coggin: What about that man who got hurt last night on overtime while unloading those sheets?

Patella: He's been on the job for a couple of months, but he tells me he wasn't familiar with the method of blocking that Zenith Metals uses. He's not hurt bad, but he'll get workmen's compensation OK.

Coggin: Sure. Now how certain are you about Farrell not finding any bottle behind the tool crib after he suspended Valenti? And are you sure you're right that there were no witnesses? You know you've got to be positive of your evidence.

Patella: OK, Ralph. I'm certain, I'm sure, I'm positive!

AFTERNOON MEETING

Three hours later, Plant Manager Burger is again in a meeting with Production Chief Polk, Quality Control Manager Peters, and Industrial Relations Manager Coggin.

Burger: Let's hear from you first, Bob, about that check on the presses and the blanker. Any clues to those burrs?

Polk: Nope. Everything is OK with the machinery, according to Engineering. They even thought I was nuts to be questioning them and making them double-check.

Burger: I can imagine. But we can't overlook anything, no matter how impossible Engineering may think it is. By the way, Ben, are the rejects still running as high this afternoon?

Peters: Higher. Line #1 is lousing up nine or ten an hour, Line #2 is ruining about a dozen, and Line #4 is burring about seven an hour.

Burger: What about Line #3?

Peters: Nothing so far. Dawson's line has been clean as a whistle. But, with Valenti's brother on the line, we can expect trouble any time.

Polk: Maybe not. Dawson's reject rates have always been a bit lower than the others'.

Burger: That so? How do you account for that?

Coggin: How about better supervision accounting for it? Dawson's men always seem to take more pride in their work than the other men do, and they really operate as a team. The other day I heard two of his men talking about one of their crew who apparently was getting careless, and they decided to straighten him out themselves, without bothering Dawson. When you get that kind of voluntary discipline, you've got real supervision.

Burger: Glad to hear that some of our men feel responsible for doing good work.

Polk: Dawson's crew is OK. One of his men will always tip me off early if they're getting low on blanks, but the night shift on that line is mighty careless. That crew left Dawson's line with only a half-hour's stack of blanks to start up with this morning.

Peters: By the way, Bob, have you heard that some of the men on the other crews are calling his men "Dawson's Darlings"? The rumor is that those shallow Cheetah panels are easier to make, and someone played favorites when they gave that production run to Dawson's crew.

Polk: That's crazy. We gave those panels to Dawson's line because this makes it easier for the Shipping Department, and they just aren't any easier to make; you know that.

Peters: I know, but that's what the men say, and I thought you'd like to be cut in on the grapevine.

Coggin: If the men think the deep panels are a harder job, maybe there's something to it. I've heard this story, too, and there's a chance the union may try to review our rates and standards one of these days.

Polk: Yeah? Well, I say nuts to it. If those items go on the agenda, then Patella might as well be running this shop. Why don't we ask the union: "How about making up for that half-hour Line #2 lost this morning while Valenti argued with Farrell about his suspension?"

Coggin: While you're asking, ask Farrell why he didn't call me before suspending Valenti yesterday. What a mess Farrell put us in!

Burger: What do you mean, Ralph?

Coggin: Just that we've got a real big grievance coming up, for sure. Patella tells me that after Farrell suspended Valenti yesterday, he went looking behind the tool crib and couldn't find any sign of a liquor bottle. Also, Patella claims there were no witnesses around when Farrell accused Valenti of drinking on the job. It's going to be impossible for Farrell to prove he wasn't acting merely on his suspicions, without evidence. And the union is sure to hit us hard with this, especially with contract negotiations coming up.

Burger: Damn it, Farrell should have known better! This isn't the first time he's been tough with a man, but he's got to learn to use better judgment. Bob, you'd better have a talk with him right away. See if anything special is chewing him. Maybe a little firm advice from you will sharpen him up.

Polk: OK, Oscar, but Farrell's a very good man, and we ought to back him up on this completely.

Coggin: If you do, you're going to have real trouble with the union. Patella says if we don't drop the charge against Valenti and reinstate him, he's going to propose a strike vote, and he claims the men will positively go out. It looks like they have a clear case against Farrell and, except for Dawson's men, a lot of them seem plenty sore. And those rejects they're producing are telling you so, loud and clear.

Polk: Oscar, we can't undercut Farrell! If we do, we're playing right into the union's hands. It's obvious that Valenti is in collusion with Patella on this, and they're framing Farrell to get themselves a hot issue for the contract negotiations. I say we should charge the union with framing Farrell and willfully producing rejects. If they try to strike, get an injunction immediately so we can keep production up and satisfy Detroit.

Burger: Not so fast, Bob. I'd rather first try to get the union off our backs before they seriously start talking about a strike. Ralph, what about that demand the local union agent told you he was going to make—something like 10 minutes' extra wash-up time? If we gave in to him on this, do you think he could hold Patella in line on this Farrell-Valenti problem?

Coggin: Probably. But you would want to find some way for Patella to save face, as well as Farrell.

Burger: You may be right, but we can't let Patella think he can go on using this sabotage technique of his. I want to mull this over some more before deciding what our answer will have to be. Meanwhile, Ben, you keep a close check on the reject rates. And you, Bob, check on the operation on Line #3 to see if there really is anything to that rumor about our favoring Dawson's crew. Ralph, see what you can find out about that extra wash-up time deal and how Patella feels about it. That's about all I can suggest for now. Let's meet again tomorrow at 10 o'clock and wind this thing up.

BURGER'S DILEMMA

The meeting breaks up and the managers go back to their respective jobs. Plant Manager Burger spends some time by himself trying to resolve the dilemma. He sees two choices facing him: (1) back up Farrell and risk a strike that might be stopped by injunction, or (2) avoid a strike by undercutting Farrell, reinstating Valenti, and asking the men to cooperate in eliminating excess rejects. He does not like either of the alternatives, and hopes he can think of some better way to get out of this jam. At least, he tells himself, he has a night to sleep on it.

Your Analysis?

Has Plant Manager Burger analyzed the situation correctly? You are invited to think through this situation for yourself and decide how you would go about solving it. You will be able to compare your results with the solutions that will be presented in Part II in Chapter 6, which will describe the Kepner-Tregoe concepts and procedures for problem analysis.

Notes

1. See "Developing Decision Makers," HBR September–October 1960, p. 115.

2. Charles H. Kepner and Benjamin B. Tregoe, *The Rational Manager*, edited with an introduction by Perrin Stryker (New York, McGraw-Hill Book Company, Inc.).

Originally published in May–June 1965
Reprint 65312

How to Analyze That Problem

Part II of a Management Exercise

PERRIN STRYKER

Executive Summary

THIS IS THE SEQUEL to the management exercise published in Chapter 5, "Can You Analyze This Problem?"

P ART I OF THIS TWO-INSTALLMENT ARTICLE on problem analysis invited readers to test their reasoning powers against the problems presented in a case history based directly on an actual situation. This case was reported to Kepner-Tregoe and Associates, whose systematic approach to problem analysis, as described in this installment, made possible the correct solution of a very puzzling situation.

Before resuming the action, I will first give a brief synopsis of what has transpired in the first installment and then introduce the characters who appear in this concluding part (all but one of whom appeared in Part I).

The Situation

In a plant making quarter panels and other parts for one of the Big Three auto companies, the Plant Manager and three key subordinates are trying to find out why burrs and rough spots are suddenly appearing on so many panels, causing them to be rejected. They strongly suspect deliberate sabotage by the operators on the production lines, who are reported to be angry over the suspension of worker Joe Valenti by a hotheaded supervisor, who accused him of drinking on the job. The shop steward threatens to call a strike if the supervisor is not reprimanded for his arbitrary action and also if Valenti is not reinstated.

The Plant Manager collects as many facts as possible in a meeting with his key subordinates, and then adjourns the meeting until the next morning. In the meanwhile, he hopes he can decide what to do. He sees two alternatives: back up the supervisor and risk a strike that might be stopped by injunction; or avoid a strike by undercutting the supervisor, reinstating Valenti, and asking the workers on the line to cooperate in eliminating the excessive rejects. The Plant Manager hopes that he can find another, better alternative, however, before the second meeting with his managers.

THE PRINCIPALS

The following short descriptions of the characters who appear in this second part of the article (the names are disguised) may be useful:

- Oscar Burger, Plant Manager—a tough manager in his late fifties; known for his willingness to listen to others; considered antiunion by the employees.

- Robert Polk, Production Chief—a hard-nosed driver, very able technically, but quick-tongued and inclined to favor certain subordinates; also considered antiunion by the employees.

- Ben Peters, Quality Control Manager—reserved, quiet, and cautious when dealing with others; extremely confident in his figures.

- Ralph Coggin, Industrial Relations Manager—a fairly typical personnel manager; sympathetic to employees; relies on human relations techniques in dealing with the union.

- Joyce Luane, Scheduling Supervisor—persistent, analytical, and systematic; has had some training in problem analysis procedure, but lacks experience.

Problem Analysis

The situation for Part II of this case opens at 9:30 a.m. on Thursday in the office of Plant Manager Burger (the next-morning meeting).

Burger: Before we begin this morning, you notice I've asked Joyce Luane, our Scheduling Supervisor, to sit in with us. She's just returned from taking a five-day course in problem solving and decision making, and I thought this would be a good chance to see if she's really learned anything. Now then, Ben, let's hear about those reject rates on the panels. How do they look this morning?

Peters: They're still way over our 2% tolerance on lines #1, #2, and #4. If anything, they're a bit higher than yesterday.

Burger: Hasn't Line #3 begun to foul up a lot of panels yet?

Peters: No signs of it, Oscar.

Burger: Bob, did Engineering check out the stamping press on Line #3? You know we wanted to track down that rumor about the stamping job on the Cheetah panels being easier than on the Panther panels.

Polk: Engineering says it's strictly rumor—there's absolutely no difference in the stamping time required on any of the four lines.

Burger: Damn . . . I thought that we might have traced this reject trouble to the presses somehow.

Coggin: You still can't say that the people on lines #1, #2, and #4 don't feel that the work on Dawson's Line #3 is easier; and if they think Dawson's crew has been favored by getting the Cheetah panels, there could be something in it.

Burger: But Engineering says no, Ralph. We can't psychoanalyze people to find out why they believe this, if they really do. More to the point, what did you find out about that wash-up time deal the local union agent plans to ask us for?

Coggin: Shop Steward Patella says he'll be glad if the workers get this extra time, but he still demands that Valenti be reinstated and that Supervisor Farrell be reprimanded. I don't think Patella would back down even if the local agent told him not to threaten a strike. And the operators really seem sore enough to walk out on us.

Burger: All right, then, that settles it. I've made up my mind. Since we've got to avoid a strike at all costs, with Detroit hounding us for all the panels we can ship, we're going to reinstate Valenti, reprimand Farrell, and also jack up the other supervisors so they'll catch any one trying to produce rejects deliberately. Then we'll ask the crews to cooperate in keeping the reject rates within our tolerance. You, Ruth, will tell Patella that if we catch him inciting people to sabotage the production lines by burring a lot of panels—just in the hope of getting a hot issue for the new contract negotiations—then we'll charge him and the union with this before the NLRB. If they threaten us with a strike, we'll get an injunction to carry us at least over the next two months of maximum output.

Polk: I'm real glad to hear you take a strong line on this, Oscar. We've been too soft with that union for a long time, in my opinion. But I don't think you ought to reprimand Farrell and reinstate Valenti. That could hurt all our supervisors.

Burger: Sorry, but that's it, Bob. Farrell was too rash in suspending Valenti without any evidence. We've got to calm the operators down and stop this damned burring trouble, or we'll have Detroit on our necks, and hard!

Coggin: I think you're doing just right, and I'm sure the crews on the lines will cooperate in licking this reject problem.

Burger: I hope so. Anyway, I can't see a better decision at this time. (*He turns to Luane.*) Now, Joyce, how did we do? What do you think of our problem solving and decision making?

Luane: I can't really say, Mr. Burger, because I'm not at all sure just what the problem is.

Burger: Well, it started out as a reject problem and then developed into a touchy union situation we've had to handle.

Polk: The basic problem, Joyce, is discipline in the shop. We've been too lax with the operators and too soft with the union.

Coggin: I'd say the real problem is our need to train the supervisors in their responsibilities. Also, we've got a communications problem if a supervisor like Farrell fails to get the message that he must notify me before taking disciplinary action.

Luane: Let's see . . . that makes six problems you have mentioned—rejects, union antagonism, shop discipline, lack of supervisory training, low morale, and poor communications.

Burger: Yes, but you could say they're really all part of one whole problem, as I see it.

Luane: One whole problem? What's that? From what I heard, it sounds like you've got a mess of problems here.

Burger: What I mean by the whole problem is managing this entire plant so everything runs on schedule and putting out what Detroit wants. Did they teach you how to solve that kind of problem in your training course?

Luane: Not exactly. But I did learn the difference between a problem and a decision, and I think some of you have been mixing these two things up, from what I have heard.

DEFINING THE PROBLEM

Let us pause here for a moment and see what these managers have been doing. First, Plant Manager Burger checked on the points of information he'd asked for at the previous meeting, and these satisfied him that he was right in assuming sabotage to be the cause of the high reject rates on the panels. He then made several decisions which he judged capable of taking care of both the reject problem and the labor difficulties.

Some of Burger's decisions seem right to Production Chief Polk, who only disputes Burger's handling of Farrell and Valenti; and all seem right to Industrial Relations Manager Coggin, who accepts Burger's reasoning completely.

Then Scheduling Supervisor Joyce Luane begins to ask some pertinent questions and finds that each manager is using the word "problem" in a different sense, without realizing it. And they have been repeatedly committing the major error in problem solving—namely, jumping to conclusions about the cause of a problem. For example, Polk says the "basic problem" is lack of discipline in the shop, and he assumes that this problem is the cause of the excessive rejects. On the other hand, Coggin sees one problem as the need for training, which he says is the cause for low morale, and he sees another problem as lack of communications, which he assumes caused Farrell's blunder, while Burger views all these failings and assumed causes as part of one big "problem of managing this entire plant."

These confusions in meaning are apparent to Luane because she has learned to distinguish problems from decisions. She sees any problem as a deviation from some standard or norm of desired performance. And to her a decision is now always a choice among various ways of getting a particular thing done or accomplished. Thus she recognizes that Coggin is really talking about a decision when he says that "our real problem is the need to train supervisors." Similarly, Luane realizes that Burger's "whole problem" is not a mere collection of failures and causes, but a statement describing his responsibility for making decisions as head of the plant. So Luane tries to clarify some of this confusion.

Luane: I suggest we agree on what we mean by a problem so we can concentrate on that, and not worry right now about any decisions or any causes. The simplest way to solve a problem is to think of it as something that's wrong, that's out of kilter, something we want to fix. If we identify that for sure, then we can begin to look for what caused it; and when we've found the cause, then we can get into decision making, which is choosing the best way to correct the cause.

Burger: But it isn't that simple, is it? We want to correct a lot of things around here, and they're usually mixed up together.

Luane: Yes, but you can't work on them all at once, and you can't solve a lot of problems by correcting just one of them.

Burger: OK, let's go along with Joyce on this, but I personally think there are times when you can solve a lot of problems by solving one key problem.

Luane: I think you'll find that the key problem is almost always at the end of a chain of other problems and causes. That is, the cause of one problem is itself a problem, and its cause is another problem, and the cause of that other problem is still another problem to be solved, and so on. It's kind of a stair-stepping sequence. Usually, if you correct the *cause* of the *basic* problem in such a sequence, the other problems and their causes will automatically disappear.

Polk: I'll buy that. If we correct the lax discipline in the shop, we'll correct the reject problem and those labor troubles, too.

Luane: Not necessarily. You've got to be certain they're connected in a problem-cause sequence. It's safer to assume that they're not connected, and then pick the problem that's most important and start analyzing from there.

Burger: All right, let's pick our most important problem and get on with this. Obviously the high reject rate on those panels is our biggest problem now. If we don't get it solved fast, at the present rate of rejects we'll be fouling up more than 2,500 panels every shift, and we can't stand for that.

Polk: That's for sure, Oscar, but after we jack up the supervisors and the press operators, and get the reject rates back in line, let's not forget to keep pushing for more discipline.

Luane: Aren't you talking now about a decision, Bob—what should be done to keep things going as you think they should?

Polk: I guess so, by your definition, but it's damned important.

Luane: I'm not doubting it, but we still haven't decided that the reject problem is our number one problem.

Coggin: If you mean the biggest immediate problem, then I'll admit it's the rejects, but they're only symptoms of bigger, more fundamental problems, in my opinion.

Burger: If we flop in delivering our quota of panels in this busy season, we can cost the company such a pile of money it makes me shudder.

Luane: What if those reject rates on the panels keep rising?

Polk: Say, haven't we got it bad enough? You know that any rejects above 5% are very serious business. We've got to hold them below 2%—no "if"s or "but"s or we can shut up shop.

Luane: OK, fair enough. I was just trying to make sure we had identified not only the most serious and urgent problem, but the one that could grow into real critical financial trouble.

Coggin: I'm still convinced that our most important problem has to do with people, especially our headaches in training and helping them communicate.

Burger: Be realistic, Ralph. If we don't correct this reject problem and produce what's required by Detroit, we may not be around to worry about *any* problems.

Luane: Let's call this reject problem our number one problem. We can list the others, too, but give them less priority right now. Next, we've got to describe this reject problem precisely, and I mean *precisely*.

Polk: Oh, so they taught you to "define the problem first"? Sounds very familiar. Next you'll be telling us to "get all the facts." I've seen a lot of these step-by-step gimmicks, but I don't believe they really work.

Luane: Matter of fact, getting all the information would just be a big waste of time. Only some of the facts would be useful to us. That's one reason I want to describe this problem precisely. Another reason is that we're going to use this specification to test any possible causes we find.

OUTLINING THE SPECIFICATION

Again let us see what these managers have been accomplishing. Luane has stated three basic concepts: a problem is a deviation from some standard of desired performance; a decision is a choice of the best way to correct the cause of a problem; and every problem has only one cause. She also has pointed out the stair-stepping process of going from one problem to its cause, which, in turn, may be a problem to be solved.

But the managers don't pay much attention to these ideas, and Polk clearly misunderstands stair-stepping, for he clings to the conclusion he earlier jumped to—that lax discipline is the cause of several problems. Industrial Relations Manager Coggin thinks "people problems" are fundamentally more important, but he accepts the priority his superiors give to the reject problem. At this point, Luane has tried to get the managers to think in terms of the urgency, seriousness, and growth trend of the problem. Having settled on the reject rate as the most important problem, they now are ready to start analyzing it.

Luane: How would you describe this reject problem, Bob?

Polk: Why, I'd say the problem is that the reject rates are way out of line.

Luane: How about you, Mr. Burger?

Burger: Let's see. I'd say it was too many burred panels.

Luane: And you, Ben? Haven't heard a peep out of you for some time now.

Peters: I guess I'd go along with Bob on the reject rates being beyond tolerance.

Luane: We'll have to get more specific. We're trying to describe this exactly. As an overall description, how about "Excessive rejects from burring on quarter panels"? Anyway, let's write that down for a starter. (*She goes to an easel blackboard and writes these words out.*) Now we have to dissect this problem in detail, getting specific facts about it in four different dimensions—*What, Where, When,* and *Extent.* (*She writes these four words down on the left side of the blackboard.*) What's more, we want to get two sets of facts opposite each of these dimensions—those that describe precisely what the problem Is and those that describe precisely what the problem Is Not. (*She writes Is and Is Not at the top of two columns of blank space.*)

Polk: What's all this for, anyway? Are we drawing a chart or something?

Luane: Sort of a map. This is the specification worksheet, and the point is to fill the Is column with only those things directly affected by the problem. In the Is Not column we will put the things that are closely related to the problem but not affected by it. You'll see why we do this in a few minutes.

Burger: OK, but I hope this doesn't take too long. Sounds kind of detailed to me.

Luane: It's pretty simple, actually. Under *What*, we can first put down "burrs" as the deviation in this Is column, and "any other complaint" in the Is Not column, since, as I understand it, there are no other complaints reported on these panels. But we can be more specific here, too. For instance, what did this deviation, "burrs," appear on? Were they on all kinds of panels?

Polk: No, Joyce, just on the Panther panels, not the Cheetah panels.

Luane: So we can put down, under *What*, the words "Panther panels" in the Is column, and "Cheetah panels" in the Is Not column. Got the idea?

Polk: I guess so, but it sounds a little too simple to me. Why bother?

Luane: The point here is we're trying to separate what the problem Is from everything that Is Not the problem. We're aiming to draw a tight line around the problem, to describe it precisely, and later you'll see how this gives us the clues to the cause of the problem.

Polk: I hope so.

Luane: Now we do the same thing for this *Where* section of the specification. Where was the deviation seen on the objects affected? Obviously, the burrs appeared on the Panther panels, so we put this down under Is. Also, where in the plant were the burrs observed?

Burger: So far, only on lines #1, #2, and #4, but with Line #3 expected to go bad any minute.

Luane: So under Is of this *Where* section we can put "lines #1, #2, and #4," and under Is Not, we can put "Line #3." Also, we have to fill in the Is Not opposite the words "Panther panels." Where didn't the burrs appear?

Polk: Nowhere else. We all know that.

Luane: I know, but we've got to make this specification as accurate as possible. We can put down "other parts" under Is Not, since we know no other parts were affected.

Polk: I can't see where we're going with all this business.

Burger: Neither can I, Bob, but let's let her finish.

Luane: Now we come to the *When* part of this specification. Here we ought to be extra careful and get exact times, if possible. Ben, what times did those reject rates start going up yesterday morning?

Peters: You mean exactly? (*He consults his papers.*) On Line #2, the first excessive rejects showed up at 9:33 a.m.; on Line #1, they appeared at 10:18; and on Line #4, at 11:23 a.m. From those times on, each of these lines turned out rejects that were far above our tolerance of 2%.

Luane: That's nice and precise. Can't tell, it may be important, so we'll put the exact times down. Now, how about the Is Not here? There were no burrs at all on lines #1, #2, and #4 before these times, and none at all on Line #3 at any time.

Burger: I think I begin to see why you use those Is and Is Not columns. It's to put off to one side all the facts you aren't going to think about in solving this problem.

Luane: No, that's not exactly why, but it will be clear as soon as we finish this specification. This last section, called *Extent*, covers the size of the problem—how big or serious it is, how many items are involved. We can put down "bad burring" and list the percentage of rejects on each line. Now what were those percentages, Ben?

Peters (consulting his papers again): On Line #2, 11% rejects. On Line #1, 17.5%, and on Line #4, 15%. That's according to final counts last night.

Luane: That leaves us only the Is Not column to fill in here, and this would cover the rejects on Line #3. We can say "Line #3 rejects" here, since they have stayed within the 2% tolerance. Now we've got the specification all filled in.

Burger: Still looks like a simple collection of facts. Is that all there is to this system?

Luane: No, Mr. Burger. Now we've got to begin analyzing this specification to dig out the cause of this problem.

Polk: You mean *now* we're finally going to start solving it?

SPOTTING THE DISTINCTION

Here we can briefly review what Luane has done in drawing up this specification. She followed a systematic outline to describe precisely both the problem and what lies outside the problem but is closely related to it. (See Exhibit I for Luane's specification worksheet.) The contrast between the Is and the Is Not not only draws a boundary

Specification Worksheet

DEVIATION: EXCESSIVE REJECTS FROM BURRING ON QUARTER PANELS

	Is	Is Not	What Is Distinctive of the *Is*?	Any Change in This?
What				
Deviation	Burrs	Any other complaint		—
Object	Panther panels	Cheetah panels	Deep draw	—
Where				
On object observed	Panther panels Lines #1, #2, & #4	Other parts Line #3	Deep draw	
When				
On object observed	Line #2 – 9:33 a.m. Line #1 – 10:18 a.m. Line #4 – 11:23 a.m.	{ Any burrs before these times on Lines #2, #1, & #4 Line #3 at any time	Stacks of Zenith's blanks began to be used at these times	New alloy in Zenith steel
Extent				
How much	Bad burring	Line #3 rejects		
How many	{ Line #2 – 11% rejects Line #1 – 17.5% " Line #4 – 15% "		Reject rates not proportional to involvement in Farrell–Valenti conflict	
Possible Causes for Test	A new alloy in Zenith's sheet steel is causing the excessive burring in the presses			

*around the problem, but strictly limits the amount of
information needed for its solution. There is no need to
"get all the facts"—only the relevant facts.*

*Note that Burger, Polk, and Peters all had different
ways of describing the reject problem at first. Also, Burger
thinks the specification looks too "detailed," while to Polk
it sounds "too simple" at one point. The separation of the
Is and the Is Not sounds strange to these managers
because, like everyone else, they have learned to think in
terms of similarities, not differences. This habit will bother
them again a little further on in this problem analysis.
Both Burger and Polk are impatient with this specification
stage because they haven't yet seen the reasoning behind
it.*

*A precise specification makes possible two logical steps
toward finding possible causes of the problem, and after
that, as Luane pointed out, it serves as a testing sheet to
identify the most likely cause. Luane now turns to the
specification on the board and introduces the managers
to the most demanding part of this analytical process.*

Luane: We're ready now to use those contrasts
between the Is and the Is Not of this specification. Whatever caused this problem produced *only* those effects we
have described on the Is side; so if one thing is affected
and another related thing is not, then there must be
something distinctive or unique about the thing affected
to set it apart from the other. If we know what is distinctive. . . .

Burger (*interrupting*): I don't see any contrast between
"burrs" and "any other complaint" in this specification,
but I do see one between "Panther panels" and "Cheetah
panels." I begin to get what you're driving at. The Panther panels are affected by the cause; the Cheetah ones

aren't. We want to find out what sets the Panther panels apart from the Cheetahs, isn't that it?

Luane: Yes, you look first for a sharp contrast between the Is and the Is Not, like the one you've spotted. Then we know there must be something distinctive about those Panther panels.

Burger: Both panels are made from the same steel sheets, so the only way you could distinguish one from the other would be by its shape. The Panther panels are a deeper draw than the Cheetah panels.

Luane: That's a distinction all right. We'll put down "deep draw" as a distinction in this *What* section of the specification. (*She writes the distinction off to one side of the blackboard.*) Now can you see any distinction in the *Where* section?

Burger: I don't see any distinction there, like in the first case. Nothing distinctive of "Panther panels" as opposed to "other parts" that I can think of. Then you've got lines #1, #2, and #4 on the Is side and Line #3 on the Is Not side, and these lines are damned similar, except that Line #4 is a slow, old-time press. But that would only distinguish Line #4 from lines #1 and #2, which isn't what you're asking for.

Luane: No, we don't want a distinction like that, between things that are together on the Is side. We're looking for what sets the Is apart from the Is Not.

Polk: How about saying that Panther panels are distinctive of those three lines on the Is side? Line #3 makes only Cheetah panels, as we said a moment ago.

Luane: We can put it down if we want to, but it's really a contrast we already have in our specification, and not a distinction. It's the same contrast we have here in the *What* section between Is and Is Not. What we want is something that really sets lines #1, #2, and #4 apart from Line #3.

Polk: Then the only distinction you have there is that same "deep draw," as we said before.

Luane: I agree. We'll put it down again in this *Where* section. Let's go and see what distinction we can find in the *When* section, where we put down the different times that the burrs showed up on lines #1, #2, and #4.

Polk: How about saying those times are all distinctly in the morning, not the afternoon?

Luane: But how does that make them distinct from Line #3, where there are no times given at all? We're looking for something distinctive associated with those times.

Peters: Wait a minute! I've got a hunch those times have something to do with the stacks of blanks delivered to the presses. I remember Adams on Line #1 told me late yesterday that the bad burrs began on his line just after using up the four stacks of blanks his area had been loaded with in the morning. And another thing—maybe those high-speed presses are just right for the shallow-draw panel that Dawson's line is stamping, but not quite right for the deep-draw Panther panels.

Polk: Come on, Ben, slow down! You know Henschel's Line #4 has an old, slow press, and he's getting a lot of burrs, so the speed can't be causing the rejects.

Peters: Not just the speed, Bob, but the speed in combination with the deep-draw panels.

Luane: Let's stick to this specification job and not jump to conclusions. I'm not knocking your hunches, Ben, for I've found they can often be useful, providing you hold them aside until you start looking for possible causes. We can make a note of them so we won't forget them later. (*She writes off to one side of the specification,*

"Burring times connected with using up the stacks of blanks," and "Press speed and deep draw combine to make burrs.")

Polk: I don't think Ben's hunch on press speeds and draws is any good, in any case. Engineering told me a while ago that they spent a lot of time examining the presses at various speeds and never found any stamping defects traceable either to press speeds or to the depth of draw.

Peters: But how about the combination of speeds and different draws? Bob, I think you've got too much confidence in Engineering.

Luane: Can we get back to this specification? Does anyone see any distinction in this *When* section?

Burger: I think Ben has a point there about the stacks of blanks on Line #1 being used up just before the bad burring started. How about the other lines?

Peters: I don't know, but we can find out.

Luane: Will it take long?

Peters: No, just a phone call. (*He reaches for the phone, gets his assistant on the line, and asks her to check the times when lines #2 and #4 used up the stacks of blanks they started out with the morning before.*)

Luane: While we're waiting, let's look for distinctions in this last section of *Extent.*

Polk: Don't see any, unless it's that "deep-draw" distinction again.

Luane: As I see it, the distinction would have to be in those rates of burring we put down here, not in the panels or the presses.

Burger: Well, you could say that the rates of burring on lines #1, #2, and #4 don't correspond very well with the ways those lines were involved with that Farrell-Valenti quarrel. I mean, Farrell's Line #2 ought to show the most burrs, and actually it shows less than the other two lines.

Coggin: Maybe the reason is that the operators on lines #1 and #4 are really madder than those on Farrell's line. Maybe Valenti has more friends on the other two lines. You can't distribute and measure feelings with percentage points, like you can with those reject figures.

Luane: Sorry to have to remind you again, Ralph, but that's jumping to a conclusion about the cause. We'd better not do this until we've finished with this specification.

Coggin: Well, I can't just sit here and let the rest of you ignore the human side of this problem. When are we going to get to that, anyway?

Luane: We'll take it up if this analysis leads us in that direction. It hasn't yet. So let's put down that distinction connected with the different rates of rejects and the different degrees of involvement with the Valenti affair. We can call this distinction, "Reject rates not proportional to involvement in Valenti conflict."

Peters (reading a note his assistant has just brought in): Here are those times we asked for. Line #2 used up its stacks of Tuesday blanks at 9:30 a.m. yesterday, and Line #4 at 11:20 a.m. That checks out, as I thought. The bad burrs started on all these lines just after they started using stacks of blanks delivered to the floor Wednesday morning.

Luane: Looks like that gives us a distinction for the *When* section. We can call it, "Stacks of Tuesday's blanks used up at these times."

Polk: But how about Line #3? Ben, did your assistant get the time that Dawson's line finished using its supply of Tuesday's blanks?

Peters: Yes. At 8:30 yesterday morning.

Polk: And no bad burring started on Line #3, so what's the importance of this distinction?

Luane: We can't tell yet, Bob, but we'll just put it down for now. That seems to complete our distinctions, unless anyone sees any more in this specification. If not, we can proceed to look for the possible causes of this problem.

SEEKING THE CAUSE

At this point these managers have presumably collected all the relevant information that describes their problem precisely and have dug out those distinctive things in the Is *facts that are characteristic marks of the problem. But they had trouble spotting the distinctions, as Luane expected. Also, one of them, Peters, introduced a couple of hunches into the discussion, exhibiting a tendency to "feel" that things are connected somehow or are important.*

Note that Luane does not completely discourage such hunches, only recommends they be set aside until later. But note, too, that Peters' reasoning about his first hunch is faulty, as Polk quickly points out, while his second hunch is simply another example of jumping to a conclusion about the cause, as Luane points out. It is Burger who seems to be the sharpest here in spotting a distinction, after stumbling at first. By this time apparently only Industrial Relations Manager Coggin is still interested in the "human side of the problem," as he puts it, but his job is, of course, most directly concerned with this angle.

Luane, by keeping the discussion on the specification, prevents a time-wasting digression. She also warns Polk against prematurely judging the last distinction (about using up Tuesday's blanks) as useless just because it doesn't

seem to fit in with another fact in the specification—
that is, the absence of serious burrs on Line #3.

Now Luane introduces the managers to a concept that
lies at the heart of problem analysis, the concept that the
cause of every problem is a change of one kind or
another.

Luane: The distinctions we've gotten out of the specification give us the areas where we can look for possible
causes of these burred panels. Let's look for any changes
we can find in any of the distinctions. What's new or different in these distinctions? We probably won't find
many. Maybe only one.

Burger: Do you mean any kind of change?

Luane: No, only those changes which have occurred
within one of these areas of distinction, or have had an
effect on one of them. We can start with that distinction
of "deep draw."

Polk: I can't believe that a change is always the cause
of a problem. It can be any little thing, or some goof-off,
or bonehead action.

Luane: Maybe those things go along with the cause,
but I think we'll find here that these burred panels are
being caused by some change. Also, Mr. Burger, I meant
to point out that we don't want to go looking for everything that's changed, or we'll be here all day. There are
things changing all over the plant all the time. But what
we want to find is any change that's in one of these areas
of distinction.

Polk: I'm not convinced, and what's more I don't see
anything changed in that "deep draw" distinction. The
deep draw is standardized on all three presses making it,
and has been for months.

Luane: OK, so there's no change there. But what about
that distinction we were going to check out in the *When*

section? What's changed about those "stacks of Tuesday's blanks used up at these times"? Anything new or different about these stacks?

Peters: Well, the shift from Tuesday's blanks to Wednesday morning's blanks would be a change.

Luane: That sounds like a real change to me. Wednesday's stacks are the new blanks the lines started to work on just before the burring started.

Burger: If that's the cause of these rejects, how do you figure it? I can see that if Wednesday's blanks were different in some way from Tuesday's, that might make them the cause of the rejects.

Luane: Let's hold off on possible causes until we're sure there aren't some more changes in these distinctions.

Polk: I can't see any more changes. I say let's get on with it and start looking for possible causes.

Luane: OK, if you want to, but are we sure there's not some change connected with that other distinction in the *Extent* section, which we put down as "rates not proportional to involvement in Valenti conflict"?

Burger: I don't see anything new or different there, unless it's the differences between those rates themselves.

Luane: I can't either, so let's go ahead and check that possible cause you suggested a moment ago, when you said yesterday's blanks might be the cause of the excessive burrs. But we should test this possible cause, not just rationalize ourselves into accepting it. If this possible cause fails to explain all the facts in this specification—that is, both the facts on the Is side and those on the Is Not side—then we can be sure it's not the actual cause. Because the actual cause would have produced exactly all those things that we put down as Is in the specification, and also would explain those things we put down as Is Not.

Burger: I assume this is what you meant when you said earlier that the specification would be used in testing the possible causes?

Luane: That's right. We can start testing against the *What* of the specification by asking, "Does the use of yesterday's blanks explain the fact that the excessive burrs appear on the Panther panels and not on the Cheetah panels?"

Polk: No, of course it doesn't. Line #3 started using Wednesday's blanks even before the other lines did, and it still hasn't produced excessive burrs on the Cheetah panels.

Luane: Well then, there goes your possible cause. It doesn't fit the first facts in our specification's Is and Is Not. We'll have to toss it out.

Burger: You mean we've got to find a possible cause that accounts for every fact in this specification?

Polk: That's what she said, Oscar. But now where does this leave us? We've run out of the only change we could find.

Luane: What this means is that our specification isn't really complete. We must have missed something somewhere. We'll have to go back and sharpen up our facts if we can.

RESPECIFYING THE PROBLEM

We can pause briefly here to point out that Luane herself was responsible for the unsatisfactory results of this first search for the cause of the problem. When she accepted the change that Burger suggested—that is, the change to Wednesday's blanks just before the bad burring started—

Luane didn't think to ask about the difference between Tuesday's and Wednesday's blanks. A shift from one day's blanks to another's is not a change if the blanks are identical. Polk saw this at once, of course, and torpedoed this possible cause, as he should have. But this error of Luane's might not have occurred if she had been more careful earlier, as we shall now see.

Luane: We can go back and look over our Is and Is Not facts in the specification, but these look pretty accurate and precise to me. I think we probably missed a distinction or change.

Peters: What about those hunches of mine? You said we might come back to them.

Luane: That's an idea. What was it you said? We wrote them down over here somewhere. Here's one, "Press speed and deep draw combine to make burrs."

Polk: That's no good, as I said before. Engineering checked that thoroughly.

Luane: Well, here's Ben's other hunch, "Burring times connected with using up the stacks of blanks."

Burger: We just tested that one out and got nowhere.

Peters: Hold everything! I think we skipped a point. We talked about yesterday's blanks, but those aren't just yesterday's blanks—they're also blanks from a new supplier, Zenith. I missed this point because we'd made some parts with the Zenith metal before we ever put it in production, and it worked fine. Besides, Zenith's metal met all our specifications. We checked the blanks again when the excessive burring first occurred yesterday, and they looked perfect going through the blanker. So we dropped this as a possibility, especially when the labor trouble looked so hot.

Luane: Then that means we should change that distinction in the *When* section of our specification to

"Stacks of *Zenith*'s blanks began to be used at these times."

Polk: How will that help? Dawson's Line #3 is also using Zenith blanks, and there's no burring there.

Luane: That's jumping to a conclusion about the cause. Let's look for a change in this revised distinction. Is there anything new or different about Zenith's sheet steel? How long have we been using it?

Polk: We signed the contract a month ago.

Peters: Yes, but we didn't get delivery right off. The first shipment didn't actually get here until two days ago.

Coggin: Matter of fact, Ben, we didn't get those Zenith sheets until late Tuesday. I know, because one of the men got hurt unloading them that evening. He wasn't familiar with the way Zenith blocks the sheets for shipment.

Luane: Let's concentrate on what's new or different in Zenith's sheets.

Peters: I think they're just the same as we got from our other sheet-steel suppliers.

Luane: Are you sure?

Peters: Pretty sure. We specified a slightly different alloy for Zenith's sheets, but not enough different to matter.

Luane: Well, anyway, the new alloy is a change in an area of distinction. What is distinctive about those burring times is that stacks of new metal began being used then, and the change here is that a slightly different metal is going into the presses. We can state the possible cause this way—"A new alloy in Zenith's sheet steel is causing the excessive burring in the presses."

Burger: Ben just said he thinks the alloy change wasn't enough to matter.

Luane: I know he did, but it was a change in an area of distinction, so it's a possible cause. We can test it against the facts in the specification. Could this change—the slightly different alloy—explain the appearance of excessive burrs in the Panther panels, but not in the Cheetah panels?

Coggin: No, it couldn't, because the Cheetah panels aren't having trouble with excessive burrs.

Polk: Hold it a moment! Maybe the alloy could explain it. It just dawned on me that Engineering did say something about those Cheetah panels a couple of months back. Something about how their shallow draw would make it easier to use a tougher alloy in the blanks. That could mean the Panther panels are fouling up on these Zenith blanks with the new alloy! Let's check it! (*He picks up the phone and calls Engineering, which immediately confirms his hypothesis.*) Engineering says the new alloy in the Zenith sheets makes the Panther panels much more likely to burr than the Cheetah panels.

Luane: Looks like you've found it, Bob. We could go on and test this out against the rest of the specification, but I'd say you've probably discovered the most likely cause of the excessive burrs. I suggest you have Engineering verify this.

Polk: That's easy. We can do it before lunch right on the lines.

Burger: What if we find this "most likely cause" isn't the answer?

Luane: Then we'll have to respecify all over again, sharpen up the facts even more, and look for other distinctions and changes. But it looks like we've really spotted the change that's causing the trouble. In this case, the new alloy is the change, the metal supplied by Zenith is the distinction, and the deep draw on lines #1, #2, and #4 is another, added distinction. In other words, the most likely cause turned out to be a change *in* a distinction *plus* a distinction.

Coggin: You mean, Joyce, we've got to go through this whole business every time in order to solve every problem?

Luane: If you don't know the cause of the problem for sure, I'd say yes. There may be some times when you can spot a change in some facts about a problem right off and hit the cause at once. Sometimes you can just go through the process mentally, for it tells you the relevant questions to ask about every problem. But you'd better check any possible cause out carefully, and you really can't check completely unless you have a complete specification of the problem in front of you. If you don't check a possible cause this way, you may be taking action on something that's not the cause at all, and waste more time than if you had specified and analyzed the problem in the first place.

Burger: Sounds logical enough. But what if you can't find a distinction or change?

Luane: If you can't find any distinction or change in your specification, then you have to dig that much harder. And at least you know where to probe. A distinction *has* to be there if the problem exists, because whatever went wrong affected some things in a certain way, and did not affect other closely related things. There's got to be at least one distinction between these two kinds of things—the Is and the Is Not—and there's *got* to be a change that works through this area of distinction to cause the problem.

Burger: I see what you mean. Anyway, if Engineering can verify this alloy change in Zenith's sheets as the cause of those excessive rejects, I'll be damned glad. My face would sure have been red if we went ahead with those decisions I came in here with this morning, all based on the assumption that the operators were to blame for the high reject rates! And it all seemed so reasonable! Now, if this alloy change is actually the cause, all we'll have to do is shift back to sheets with the old alloy formula.

Coggin: But there's still that labor problem we haven't touched yet. When do we get around to analyzing that Farrell-Valenti trouble for a solution? And we've still got to calm Patella down somehow.

Polk: I think those problems don't need to be analyzed. We know what touched off the Farrell-Valenti trouble; we know why Patella is giving us trouble. What's got to be done now is to make some decisions. All that's needed is some straight talk. Tell the crews the facts and to get on with the job, and tell Patella to pipe down or you'll report him for attempted sabotage.

Burger: Wait a minute, Bob. Maybe we'd better first try to analyze that Farrell-Valenti trouble a little more systematically. There could be something else to it. Joyce, why not take a crack at it and then let me know what you come up with? Meanwhile, Bob, you'd better make some arrangements to start reclaiming those rejects as fast as possible. We'll need them all if Detroit asks us for what I think they will.

The meeting ends with Burger and Polk leaving together, the others following them out.

Conclusion

In these concluding exchanges we see that the analysis has clearly uncovered a cause which none of the managers were thinking of when they began, and which was actually verified as the cause. Note that the clue to the change that caused the trouble did not appear until Luane went back to the specification and sharpened up one of the distinctions. It was the point about Zenith's steel sheets that finally jogged Polk into recalling the possible effects of a deep draw on blanks made of the new alloy. Had Luane been more expert in the Kepner-Tregoe analysis procedure, the respecification might not have been necessary.

As it was, this solution turned out to be one of the more difficult kinds—for it involved, as Luane pointed out, a change in a distinction *plus* a second distinction. This second distinction was an essential condition (the deep draw) that had to occur before the particular change (the new alloy) could take effect and burr the panels.

Without a precise specification and careful analysis, only time-wasting guesswork and luck could have arrived at the most likely explanation of this problem. More important, this analysis prevented the Plant Manager from taking action that could have produced a more serious problem than the one he was trying to solve. Also, it should be noted that the managers did not automatically become expert problem-analyzers in going through this experience. They are still likely to jump to conclusions, as Polk did toward the end when he quickly prescribed actions to be taken on Coggin's labor problems without knowing their causes. It takes time to change a manager's thinking habits into a systematic approach to problem analysis.

> *Sherlock Holmes: "It's quite a three-pipe problem."*
> —Sir Arthur Conan Doyle

Originally published in July–August 1965
Reprint 65412

The Hidden Traps in
Decision Making

JOHN S. HAMMOND, RALPH L. KEENEY,
AND HOWARD RAIFFA

Executive Summary

BAD DECISIONS can often be traced back to the way
the decisions were made—the alternatives were not
clearly defined, the right information was not collected,
the costs and benefits were not accurately weighed. But
sometimes the fault lies not in the decision-making process but rather in the mind of the decision maker. The
way the human brain works can sabotage the choices
we make.

John Hammond, Ralph Keeney, and Howard Raiffa
examine eight psychological traps that are particularly
likely to affect the way we make business decisions: The
anchoring trap leads us to give disproportionate weight
to the first information we receive. The *status-quo trap*
biases us toward maintaining the current situation—even
when better alternatives exist. The *sunk-cost trap* inclines
us to perpetuate the mistakes of the past. The *confirming-*

evidence trap leads us to seek out information supporting an existing predilection and to discount opposing information. The *framing trap* occurs when we misstate a problem, undermining the entire decision-making process. The *overconfidence trap* makes us overestimate the accuracy of our forecasts. The *prudence trap* leads us to be overcautious when we make estimates about uncertain events. And the *recallability trap* leads us to give undue weight to recent, dramatic events.

The best way to avoid all the traps is awareness—forewarned is forearmed. But executives can also take other simple steps to protect themselves and their organizations form the various kinds of mental lapses. The authors show how to take action to ensure that important business decisions are sound and reliable.

MAKING DECISIONS is the most important job of any executive. It's also the toughest and the riskiest. Bad decisions can damage a business and a career, sometimes irreparably. So where do bad decisions come from? In many cases, they can be traced back to the way the decisions were made—the alternatives were not clearly defined, the right information was not collected, the costs and benefits were not accurately weighed. But sometimes the fault lies not in the decision-making process but rather in the mind of the decision maker. The way the human brain works can sabotage our decisions.

Researchers have been studying the way our minds function in making decisions for half a century. This research, in the laboratory and in the field, has revealed that we use unconscious routines to cope with the complexity inherent in most decisions. These routines, known as *heuristics*, serve us well in most situations. In judging distance, for example, our minds frequently rely on a heuristic that equates clarity with proximity. The clearer an object appears, the closer we judge it to be. The fuzzier it appears, the farther away we assume it must be. This simple mental shortcut helps us to make the continuous stream of distance judgments required to navigate the world.

Yet, like most heuristics, it is not foolproof. On days that are hazier than normal, our eyes will tend to trick our minds into thinking that things are more distant than they actually are. Because the resulting distortion poses few dangers for most of us, we can safely ignore it. For airline pilots, though, the distortion can be catastrophic. That's why pilots are trained to use objective measures of distance in addition to their vision.

Researchers have identified a whole series of such flaws in the way we think in making decisions. Some, like the heuristic for clarity, are sensory misperceptions. Others take the form of biases. Others appear simply as irrational anomalies in our thinking. What makes all these traps so dangerous is their invisibility. Because they are hardwired into our thinking process, we fail to recognize them—even as we fall right into them.

For executives, whose success hinges on the many day-to-day decisions they make or approve, the psychological traps are especially dangerous. They can undermine everything from new-product development to acquisition and divestiture strategy to succession planning. While no one can rid his or her mind of these ingrained flaws, anyone can follow the lead of airline pilots and learn to understand the traps and compensate for them.

In this article, we examine a number of well-documented psychological traps that are particularly likely to undermine business decisions. In addition to reviewing the causes and manifestations of these traps, we offer some specific ways managers can guard against them. It's important to remember, though, that the best defense is always awareness. Executives who attempt to familiarize themselves with these traps and the diverse forms they take will be better able to ensure that the decisions they make are sound and that the recommendations proposed by subordinates or associates are reliable.

The Anchoring Trap

How would you answer these two questions?

Is the population of Turkey greater than 35 million?

What's your best estimate of Turkey's population?

If you're like most people, the figure of 35 million cited in the first question (a figure we chose arbitrarily) influenced your answer to the second question. Over the years, we've posed those questions to many groups of people. In half the cases, we used 35 million in the first question; in the other half, we used 100 million. Without fail, the answers to the second question increase by many millions when the larger figure is used in the first question. This simple test illustrates the common and often pernicious mental phenomenon known as *anchoring*. When considering a decision, the mind gives disproportionate weight to the first information it receives. Initial impressions, estimates, or data anchor subsequent thoughts and judgments.

Anchors take many guises. They can be as simple and seemingly innocuous as a comment offered by a colleague or a statistic appearing in the morning newspaper. They can be as insidious as a stereotype about a person's skin color, accent, or dress. In business, one of the most common types of anchors is a past event or trend. A marketer attempting to project the sales of a product for the coming year often begins by looking at the sales volumes for past years. The old numbers become anchors, which the forecaster then adjusts based on other factors. This approach, while it may lead to a reasonably accurate estimate, tends to give too much weight to past events and not enough weight to other factors. In situations characterized by rapid changes in the marketplace, historical anchors can lead to poor forecasts and, in turn, misguided choices.

Because anchors can establish the terms on which a decision will be made, they are often used as a bargaining tactic by savvy negotiators. Consider the experience of a large consulting firm that was searching for new office space in San Francisco. Working with a commercial real-estate broker, the firm's partners identified a building that met all their criteria, and they set up a meeting with the building's owners. The owners opened the meeting by laying out the terms of a proposed contract: a ten-year lease; an initial monthly price of $2.50 per square foot; annual price increases at the prevailing inflation rate; all interior improvements to be the tenant's responsibility; an option for the tenant to extend the lease for ten additional years under the same terms. Although the price was at the high end of current market rates, the consultants made a relatively modest counteroffer. They proposed an initial price in the midrange of market rates and asked the owners to share in the renovation expenses, but they accepted all the other terms. The consultants could have been much more aggressive and creative in their counterproposal—reducing the initial price to the low end of market rates, adjusting rates biennially rather than annually, putting a cap on the increases, defining different terms for extending the lease, and so forth—but their thinking was guided by the owners' initial proposal. The consultants had fallen into the anchoring trap, and as a result, they ended up paying a lot more for the space than they had to.

WHAT CAN YOU DO ABOUT IT?

The effect of anchors in decision making has been documented in thousands of experiments. Anchors influence the decisions not only of managers, but also of accountants and engineers, bankers and lawyers, consultants and stock analysts. No one can avoid their influence; they're just too widespread. But managers who are aware of the dangers of anchors can reduce their impact by using the following techniques:

Decision makers display a strong bias toward alternatives that perpetuate the status quo.

- Always view a problem from different perspectives. Try using alternative starting points and approaches rather than sticking with the first line of thought that occurs to you.

- Think about the problem on your own before consulting others in order to avoid becoming anchored by their ideas.

- Be open minded. Seek information and opinions from a variety of people to widen your frame of reference and to push your mind in fresh directions.

- Be careful to avoid anchoring your advisers, consultants, and others from whom you solicit information and counsel. Tell them as little as possible about your own ideas, estimates, and tentative decisions. If you reveal too much, your own preconceptions may simply come back to you.

- Be particularly wary of anchors in negotiations. Think through your position before any negotiation begins in order to avoid being anchored by the other party's initial proposal. At the same time, look for opportunities to use anchors to your own advantage—if you're the seller, for example, suggest a high, but defensible, price as an opening gambit.

The Status-Quo Trap

We all like to believe that we make decisions rationally and objectively. But the fact is, we all carry biases, and those biases influence the choices we make. Decision makers display, for example, a strong bias toward alternatives that perpetuate the status quo. On a broad scale, we can see this tendency whenever a radically new product is introduced. The first automobiles, revealingly called "horseless carriages," looked very much like the buggies they replaced. The first "electronic newspapers" appearing on the World Wide Web looked very much like their print precursors.

On a more familiar level, you may have succumbed to this bias in your personal financial decisions. People sometimes, for example, inherit shares of stock that they would never have bought themselves. Although it would be a straightforward, inexpensive proposition to sell those shares and put the money into a different investment, a surprising number of people don't sell. They find the status quo comfortable, and they avoid taking action that would upset it. "Maybe I'll rethink it later," they say. But "later" is usually never.

The source of the status-quo trap lies deep within our psyches, in our desire to protect our egos from damage. Breaking from the status quo means taking action, and when we take action, we take responsibility, thus opening ourselves to criticism and to regret. Not surprisingly, we naturally look for reasons to do nothing. Sticking with the status quo represents, in most cases, the safer course because it puts us at less psychological risk.

Many experiments have shown the magnetic attraction of the status quo. In one, a group of people were randomly given one of two gifts of approximately the same value—half received a mug, the other half a Swiss chocolate bar. They were then told that they could easily exchange the gift they received for the other gift. While you might expect that about half would have wanted to make the exchange, only one in ten actually did. The status quo exerted its power even though it had been arbitrarily established only minutes before.

Other experiments have shown that the more choices you are given, the more pull the status quo has. More people will, for instance, choose the status quo when there are two alternatives to it rather than one: A and B instead of just A. Why? Choosing between A and B requires additional effort; selecting the status quo avoids that effort.

In business, where sins of commission (doing something) tend to be punished much more severely than sins of omission (doing nothing), the status quo holds a particularly strong attraction. Many mergers, for example, founder because the acquiring company avoids taking swift action to impose a new, more appropriate management structure on the acquired company. "Let's not rock the boat right now," the typical reasoning goes. "Let's wait until the situation stabilizes." But as time passes, the existing structure becomes more entrenched, and altering it becomes harder, not easier. Having failed to seize the occasion when change would have been expected, management finds itself stuck with the status quo.

WHAT CAN YOU DO ABOUT IT?

First of all, remember that in any given decision, maintaining the status quo may indeed be the best choice, but you don't want to choose it just because it is comfortable. Once you become aware of the status-quo trap, you can use these techniques to lessen its pull:

- Always remind yourself of your objectives and examine how they would be served by the status quo. You may find that elements of the current situation act as barriers to your goals.

- Never think of the status quo as your only alternative. Identify other options and use them as counterbalances, carefully evaluating all the pluses and minuses.

- Ask yourself whether you would choose the status-quo alternative if, in fact, it weren't the status quo.

- Avoid exaggerating the effort or cost involved in switching from the status quo.

- Remember that the desirability of the status quo will change over time. When comparing alternatives, always evaluate them in terms of the future as well as the present.

- If you have several alternatives that are superior to the status quo, don't default to the status quo just because you're having a hard time picking the best alternative. Force yourself to choose.

The Sunk-Cost Trap

Another of our deep-seated biases is to make choices in a way that justifies past choices, even when the past choices no longer seem valid. Most of us have fallen into this trap. We may have refused, for example, to sell a stock or a mutual fund at a loss, forgoing other, more attractive investments. Or we may have poured enormous effort into improving the performance of an employee whom we knew we shouldn't have hired in the first place. Our past decisions become what economists term *sunk costs*—old investments of time or money that are now irrecoverable. We know, rationally, that sunk costs are irrelevant to the present decision, but nevertheless they prey on our minds, leading us to make inappropriate decisions.

Why can't people free themselves from past decisions? Frequently, it's because they are unwilling, consciously or not, to admit to a mistake. Acknowledging a poor decision in one's personal life may be purely a private matter, involving only one's self-esteem, but in business, a bad decision is often a very public matter, inviting critical comments from colleagues or bosses. If you fire a poor performer whom you hired, you're making a public admission of poor judgment. It seems psychologically safer to let him or her stay on, even though that choice only compounds the error.

The sunk-cost bias shows up with disturbing regularity in banking, where it can have particularly dire consequences. When a borrower's business runs into trouble, a lender will often advance additional funds in hopes of providing the business with some breathing room to recover. If the business does have a good chance of coming back, that's a wise investment. Otherwise, it's just throwing good money after bad.

One of us helped a major U.S. bank recover after it made many bad loans to foreign businesses. We found that the bankers responsible for originating the problem loans were far more likely to advance additional funds—repeatedly, in many cases—than were bankers who took over the accounts after the original loans were made. Too often, the original bankers' strategy—and loans—ended in failure. Having been trapped by an escalation of commitment, they had tried, consciously or unconsciously, to protect their earlier, flawed decisions. They had fallen victim to the sunk-cost bias. The bank finally solved the problem by instituting a policy requiring that a loan be immediately reassigned to another banker as soon as any problem arose. The new banker was able to take a fresh, unbiased look at the merit of offering more funds.

Sometimes a corporate culture reinforces the sunk-cost trap. If the penalties for making a decision that leads to an unfavorable outcome are overly severe, managers will be motivated to let failed projects drag on endlessly—in the vain hope that they'll somehow be able to transform them into successes. Executives should recognize that, in an uncertain world where unforeseeable events are common, good decisions can sometimes lead to bad outcomes. By acknowledging that some good ideas will end in failure, executives will encourage people to cut their losses rather than let them mount.

WHAT CAN YOU DO ABOUT IT?

For all decisions with a history, you will need to make a conscious effort to set aside any sunk costs—whether psychological or economic—that will muddy your thinking about the choice at hand. Try these techniques:

- Seek out and listen carefully to the views of people who were uninvolved with the earlier decisions and who are hence unlikely to be committed to them.

- Examine why admitting to an earlier mistake distresses you. If the problem lies in your own wounded self-esteem, deal with it head-on. Remind yourself that even smart choices can have bad consequences, through no fault of the original decision maker, and that even the best and most experienced managers are not immune to errors in judgment. Remember the wise words of Warren Buffet: "When you find yourself in a hole, the best thing you can do is stop digging."

- Be on the lookout for the influence of sunk-cost biases in the decisions and recommendations made by your subordinates. Reassign responsibilities when necessary.

- Don't cultivate a failure-fearing culture that leads employees to perpetuate their mistakes. In rewarding people, look at the quality of their decision making (taking into account what was known at the time their decisions were made), not just the quality of the outcomes.

The Confirming-Evidence Trap

Imagine that you're the president of a successful mid-sized U.S. manufacturer considering whether to call off a planned plant expansion. For a while you've been concerned that your company won't be able to sustain the rapid pace of growth of its exports. You fear that the value of the U.S. dollar will strengthen in coming months, making your goods more costly for overseas consumers and dampening demand. But before you put the brakes on the plant expansion, you decide to call up an acquaintance, the chief executive of a similar company that recently mothballed a new factory, to check her reasoning. She presents a strong case that other currencies are about to weaken significantly against the dollar. What do you do?

You'd better not let that conversation be the clincher, because you've probably just fallen victim to the confirming-evidence bias. This bias leads us to seek out information that supports our existing instinct or point of view while avoiding information that contradicts it. What, after all, did you expect your acquaintance to give, other than a strong argument in favor of her own decision? The confirming-evidence bias not only affects where we go to collect evidence but also how we interpret the evidence we do receive, leading us to give too much weight to supporting information and too little to conflicting information.

We tend to subconsciously decide what to do before figuring out why we want to do it.

In one psychological study of this phenomenon, two groups—one opposed to and one supporting capital punishment—each read two reports of carefully conducted research on the effectiveness of the death penalty as a deterrent to crime. One report concluded that the death penalty was effective; the other concluded it was not. Despite being exposed to solid scientific information supporting counterarguments, the members of both groups became even more convinced of the validity of their own position after reading both reports. They automatically accepted the supporting information and dismissed the conflicting information.

There are two fundamental psychological forces at work here. The first is our tendency to subconsciously decide what we want to do before we figure out why we want to do it. The second is our inclination to be more engaged by things we like than by things we dislike—a tendency well documented even in babies. Naturally, then, we are drawn to information that supports our subconscious leanings.

WHAT CAN YOU DO ABOUT IT?

It's not that you shouldn't make the choice you're subconsciously drawn to. It's just that you want to be sure it's the smart choice. You need to put it to the test. Here's how:

- Always check to see whether you are examining all the evidence with equal rigor. Avoid the tendency to accept confirming evidence without question.

- Get someone you respect to play devil's advocate, to argue against the decision you're contemplating. Better yet, build the counterarguments yourself. What's the strongest reason to do something else? The second strongest reason? The third? Consider the position with an open mind.

- Be honest with yourself about your motives. Are you really gathering information to help you make a smart choice, or are you just looking for evidence confirming what you think you'd like to do?

- In seeking the advice of others, don't ask leading questions that invite confirming evidence. And if you find that an adviser always seems to support your point of view, find a new adviser. Don't surround yourself with yes-men.

The Framing Trap

The first step in making a decision is to frame the question. It's also one of the most dangerous steps. The way a problem is framed can profoundly influence the choices you make. In a case involving automobile insurance, for example, framing made a $200 million difference. To reduce insurance costs, two neighboring states, New Jersey and Pennsylvania, made similar changes in their laws. Each state gave drivers a new option: by accepting a limited right to sue, they could lower their premiums. But the two states framed the choice in very different ways: in New Jersey, you automatically got the limited right to sue unless you specified otherwise; in Pennsylvania, you got the full right to sue unless you specified otherwise. The different frames established different status quos, and, not surprisingly, most consumers defaulted to the status quo. As a result, in New Jersey about 80% of drivers chose the limited right to sue, but in Pennsylvania only 25% chose it. Because of the way it framed the choice, Pennsylvania failed to gain approximately $200 million in expected insurance and litigation savings.

The framing trap can take many forms, and as the insurance example shows, it is often closely related to other psychological traps. A frame can establish the status quo or introduce an anchor. It can highlight sunk costs or lead you toward confirming evidence. Decision researchers have documented two types of frames that distort decision making with particular frequency:

FRAMES AS GAINS VERSUS LOSSES

In a study patterned after a classic experiment by decision researchers Daniel Kahneman and Amos Tversky, one of us posed the following problem to a group of insurance professionals:

> *You are a marine property adjuster charged with minimizing the loss of cargo on three insured barges that sank yesterday off the coast of Alaska. Each barge holds $200,000 worth of cargo, which will be lost if not salvaged within 72 hours. The owner of a local marine-salvage company gives you two options, both of which will cost the same:*
>
> *Plan A: This plan will save the cargo of one of the three barges, worth $200,000.*
>
> *Plan B: This plan has a one-third probability of saving the cargo on all three barges, worth $600,000, but has a two-thirds probability of saving nothing.*
>
> *Which plan would you choose?*

If you are like 71% of the respondents in the study, you chose the "less risky" Plan A, which will save one barge for sure. Another group in the study, however, was asked to choose between alternatives C and D:

Plan C: This plan will result in the loss of two of the three cargoes, worth $400,000.

Plan D: This plan has a two-thirds probability of resulting in the loss of all three cargoes and the entire $600,000 but has a one-third probability of losing no cargo.

Faced with this choice, 80% of these respondents preferred Plan D.

The pairs of alternatives are, of course, precisely equivalent—Plan A is the same as Plan C, and Plan B is the same as Plan D—they've just been framed in different ways. The strikingly different responses reveal that people are risk averse when a problem is posed in terms of gains (barges saved) but risk seeking when a problem is posed in terms of avoiding losses (barges lost). Furthermore, they tend to adopt the frame as it is presented to them rather than restating the problem in their own way.

FRAMING WITH DIFFERENT REFERENCE POINTS

The same problem can also elicit very different responses when frames use different reference points. Let's say you have $2,000 in your checking account and you are asked the following question:

Would you accept a fifty-fifty chance of either losing $300 or winning $500?

Would you accept the chance? What if you were asked this question:

Would you prefer to keep your checking account balance of $2,000 or to accept a fifty-fifty chance of having either $1,700 or $2,500 in your account?

Once again, the two questions pose the same problem. While your answers to both questions should, rationally speaking, be the same, studies have shown that many people would refuse the fifty-fifty chance in the first question but accept it in the second. Their different reactions result from the different reference points presented in the two frames. The first frame, with its reference point of zero, emphasizes incremental gains and losses, and the thought of losing triggers a conservative response in many people's minds. The second frame, with its reference point of $2,000, puts things into perspective by emphasizing the real financial impact of the decision.

WHAT CAN YOU DO ABOUT IT?

A poorly framed problem can undermine even the best-considered decision. But any adverse effect of framing can be limited by taking the following precautions:

- Don't automatically accept the initial frame, whether it was formulated by you or by someone else. Always try to reframe the problem in various ways. Look for distortions caused by the frames.

- Try posing problems in a neutral, redundant way that combines gains and losses or embraces different reference points. For example: *Would you accept a fifty-fifty chance of either losing $300, resulting in a bank balance of $1,700, or winning $500, resulting in a bank balance of $2,500?*

- Think hard throughout your decision-making process about the framing of the problem. At points throughout the process, particularly near the end, ask yourself how your thinking might change if the framing changed.

- When others recommend decisions, examine the way they framed the problem. Challenge them with different frames.

Estimating and Forecasting Traps

Most of us are adept at making estimates about time, distance, weight, and volume. That's because we're constantly making judgments about these variables and getting quick feedback about the accuracy of those judgments. Through daily practice, our minds become finely calibrated.

Making estimates or forecasts about uncertain events, however, is a different matter. While managers continually make such estimates and forecasts, they rarely get clear feedback about their accuracy. If you judge, for example, that the likelihood of the price of oil falling to less than $15 a barrel one year hence is about 40% and the price does indeed fall to that level, you can't tell whether you were right or wrong about the probability you estimated. The only way to gauge your accuracy would be to keep track of many, many similar judgments to see if, after the fact, the events you thought had a 40% chance of occurring actually did occur 40% of the time. That would require a great deal of data, carefully

Even though most of us are not very good at making estimates, we tend to be overconfident about our accuracy—which can lead to bad decisions.

tracked over a long period of time. Weather forecasters and bookmakers have the opportunities and incentives to maintain such records, but the rest of us don't. As a result, our minds never become calibrated for making estimates in the face of uncertainty.

All of the traps we've discussed so far can influence the way we make decisions when confronted with uncertainty. But there's another set of traps that can have a particularly distorting effect in uncertain situations because they cloud our ability to assess probabilities. Let's look at three of the most common of these uncertainty traps:

THE OVERCONFIDENCE TRAP

Even though most of us are not very good at making estimates or forecasts, we actually tend to be overconfident about our accuracy. That can lead to errors in judgment and, in turn, bad decisions. In one series of tests, people were asked to forecast the next week's closing value for the Dow Jones Industrial Average. To account for uncertainty, they were then asked to estimate a range within which the closing value would likely fall. In picking the top number of the range, they were asked to choose a high estimate they thought had only a 1% chance of being exceeded by the closing value. Similarly, for the bottom end, they were told to pick a low estimate for which they thought there would be only a 1% chance of the closing value falling below it. If they were good at judging their forecasting accuracy, you'd expect the participants to be wrong only about 2% of the time. But hundreds of tests have shown that the actual Dow Jones averages fell outside the forecast ranges 20% to 30% of the time. Overly confident about the accuracy of their predictions, most people set too narrow a range of possibilities.

Think of the implications for business decisions, in which major initiatives and investments often hinge on ranges of estimates. If managers underestimate the high end or overestimate the low end of a crucial variable, they may miss attractive opportunities or expose themselves to far greater risk than they realize. Much money has been wasted on ill-fated product-development projects because managers did not accurately account for the possibility of market failure.

THE PRUDENCE TRAP

Another trap for forecasters takes the form of overcautiousness, or prudence. When faced with high-stakes decisions, we tend to adjust our estimates or forecasts "just to be on the safe side." Many years ago, for example, one of the Big Three U.S. automakers was deciding how many of a new-model car to produce in anticipation of its busiest sales season. The market-planning department, responsible for the decision, asked other departments to supply forecasts of key variables such as anticipated sales, dealer inventories, competitor actions, and costs. Knowing the purpose of the estimates, each department slanted its forecast to favor building more cars—"just to be safe." But the market planners took the numbers at face value and then made their own "just to be safe" adjustments. Not surprisingly, the number of cars produced far exceeded demand, and the company took six months to sell off the surplus, resorting in the end to promotional pricing.

Policymakers have gone so far as to codify overcautiousness in formal decision procedures. An extreme

example is the methodology of "worst-case analysis,"
which was once popular in the design of weapons systems and is still used in certain engineering and regula-
tory settings. Using this approach, engineers designed
weapons to operate
A dramatic or traumatic under the worst pos-
event in your own life can also sible combination of
distort your thinking. circumstances, even
though the odds of
those circumstances actually coming to pass were
infinitesimal. Worst-case analysis added enormous costs
with no practical benefit (in fact, it often backfired by
touching off an arms race), proving that too much prudence can sometimes be as dangerous as too little.

THE RECALLABILITY TRAP

Even if we are neither overly confident nor unduly prudent, we can still fall into a trap when making estimates
or forecasts. Because we frequently base our predictions
about future events on our memory of past events, we
can be overly influenced by dramatic events—those that
leave a strong impression on our memory. We all, for
example, exaggerate the probability of rare but catastrophic occurrences such as plane crashes because they
get disproportionate attention in the media. A dramatic
or traumatic event in your own life can also distort your
thinking. You will assign a higher probability to traffic
accidents if you have passed one on the way to work, and
you will assign a higher chance of someday dying of can-
cer yourself if a close friend has died of the disease.

In fact, anything that distorts your ability to recall
events in a balanced way will distort your probability
assessments. In one experiment, lists of well-known men

and women were read to different groups of people. Unbeknownst to the subjects, each list had an equal number of men and women, but on some lists the men were more famous than the women while on others the women were more famous. Afterward, the participants were asked to estimate the percentages of men and women on each list. Those who had heard the list with the more famous men thought there were more men on the list, while those who had heard the one with the more famous women thought there were more women.

Corporate lawyers often get caught in the recallability trap when defending liability suits. Their decisions about whether to settle a claim or take it to court usually hinge on their assessments of the possible outcomes of a trial. Because the media tend to aggressively publicize massive damage awards (while ignoring other, far more common trial outcomes), lawyers can overestimate the probability of a large award for the plaintiff. As a result, they offer larger settlements than are actually warranted.

WHAT CAN YOU DO ABOUT IT?

The best way to avoid the estimating and forecasting traps is to take a very disciplined approach to making forecasts and judging probabilities. For each of the three traps, some additional precautions can be taken:

- To reduce the effects of overconfidence in making estimates, always start by considering the extremes, the low and high ends of the possible range of values. This will help you avoid being anchored by an initial estimate. Then challenge your estimates of the extremes. Try to imagine circumstances where the actual figure would fall below your low or above your high, and adjust your range accordingly. Challenge the estimates of your subordinates and advisers in a similar fashion. They're also susceptible to overconfidence.

- To avoid the prudence trap, always state your estimates honestly and explain to anyone who will be using them that they have not been adjusted. Emphasize the need for honest input to anyone who will be supplying you with estimates. Test estimates over a reasonable range to assess their impact. Take a second look at the more sensitive estimates.

- To minimize the distortion caused by variations in recallability, carefully examine all your assumptions to ensure they're not unduly influenced by your memory. Get actual statistics whenever possible. Try not to be guided by impressions.

Forewarned Is Forearmed

When it comes to business decisions, there's rarely such a thing as a no-brainer. Our brains are always at work, sometimes, unfortunately, in ways that hinder rather than help us. At every stage of the decision-making process, misperceptions, biases, and other tricks of the mind can influence the choices we make. Highly complex and important decisions are the most prone to distortion because they tend to involve the most assumptions, the most estimates, and the most inputs from the most people. The higher the stakes, the higher the risk of being caught in a psychological trap.

The traps we've reviewed can all work in isolation. But, even more dangerous, they can work in concert, amplifying one another. A dramatic first impression might anchor our thinking, and then we might selectively seek out confirming evidence to justify our initial inclination. We make a hasty decision, and that decision establishes a new status quo. As our sunk costs mount, we become trapped, unable to find a propitious time to seek out a new and possibly better course. The psychological miscues cascade, making it harder and harder to choose wisely.

As we said at the outset, the best protection against all psychological traps—in isolation or in combination—is awareness. Forewarned is forearmed. Even if you can't eradicate the distortions ingrained into the way your mind works, you can build tests and disciplines into your decision-making process that can uncover errors in thinking before they become errors in judgment. And taking action to understand and avoid psychological traps can have the added benefit of increasing your confidence in the choices you make.

For further discussions of decision traps, see: J. Edward Russo and Paul J. H. Schoemaker, Decision Traps: The Ten Barriers to Brilliant Decision Making and How to Overcome Them *(New York: Simon & Schuster, 1989) and Max Bazerman,* Judgment in Managerial Decision Making *(New York: John Wiley & Sons, fourth edition, 1998).*

Originally published in September–October 1998
Reprint 98505

When to Trust Your Gut

ALDEN M. HAYASHI

Executive Summary

MANY TOP EXECUTIVES say they routinely make big decisions without relying on any logical analysis. Instead, they call upon their "intuition," "gut instinct," "hunches," or "inner voice"—but they can't describe the process much more than that.

What exactly is gut instinct? In this article, author Alden Hayashi interviews top executives from companies such as America Online and Johnson and Johnson to find out how they make decisions. Hayashi also presents the research of leading scientists who suggest that our emotions and feelings might not only be important in our intuitive ability to make good decisions but may actually be essential. Specifically, one theory contends that our emotions help us filter various options quickly, even if we're not consciously aware of the screening. Other research suggests that professional judgment can often

169

be reduced to patterns and rules; indeed, truly inspired decisions seem to require an ability to see similar patterns across disparate fields. A CEO who possesses that ability can craft a perfect strategy by detecting patterns that others either overlook or mistake for random noise.

But various traits of human nature can easily cloud our intuitive decision making. One potential pitfall is our tendency to see patterns where none exist. Thus, continual self-checking and feedback are crucial, and some organizations have made these processes part of their corporate culture.

THE INTUITIVE INSIGHT that would save Chrysler in the 1990s came to Bob Lutz, then the company's president, during a weekend drive. On a warm day in 1988, Lutz took his Cobra roadster for a spin. As he raced along the roads in southeastern Michigan, he tried to relax, pushing aside what critics had been saying about Chrysler—that the company was brain-dead, technologically dated, and uninspired and that it lagged dangerously behind not only the Japanese automakers but also General Motors and Ford.

Ironically, Lutz found it difficult to enjoy himself precisely *because* he was finding the drive so pleasurable. "I felt guilty: there I was, the president of Chrysler, driving this great car that had such a strong Ford association," he says, referring to the original Cobra's Ford V-8 engine. In fact, Lutz's strong sense of corporate loyalty had earlier led him to remove the "Powered by Ford" plaques from his car. Still, the guilt needled him, and on this drive he began wondering about replacing the Cobra's engine with one from Chrysler. Perhaps then he could enjoy his beloved sports car in peace. But he quickly realized that Chrysler did not have a V-8 engine that was up to snuff. If he made the switch, the car would lose considerable performance. "Chrysler was way, way, way behind," he remembers admitting to himself.

Soon Lutz's mind was racing. Didn't Chrysler have a powerful ten-cylinder engine in development for its new pickup truck? Could that be the answer? And, wait, wasn't Chrysler also building a five-speed, heavy-duty manual transmission for that truck? Why not co-opt those monster parts for a sexy, expensive, two-seat concept sports car that would be as revolutionary as the Cobra had been in the 1960s? Wouldn't that silence everyone who had written off Chrysler?

That Monday, Lutz leapt into action, enlisting important allies at Chrysler to develop a muscular, outrageous sports car that would turn heads and stop traffic. After seeing a full-size clay model of the car—later to become the Dodge Viper—Lutz was all the more determined. But the naysayers were many. Chrysler's bean counters were arguing that the $80 million investment would be better spent elsewhere, perhaps to pay down the company's debt or refurbish plants. The sales force warned that no U.S. automaker had ever succeeded in selling a $50,000 car. At the time, Dodge cars were priced under $20,000, and customers were mainly blue-collar workers. But Lutz persevered, pushing the project forward with unwavering commitment. Amazingly, he had no market research to support him, just his gut instincts.

The Dodge Viper became a smashing success. It single-handedly changed the public's perception of Chrysler, dramatically boosting company morale and providing the momentum that the company desperately lacked, ultimately spurring its dramatic turnaround in the 1990s. In hindsight, the Viper was exactly what Chrysler (now Daimler-Chrysler) needed; it was the right car at the right time. But how could Lutz have been so certain about that?

Lutz, now CEO of Exide Technologies, the $3 billion manufacturer of car batteries, has trouble describing exactly how he made one of the most critical decisions of his career. "It was this subconscious, visceral feeling. And it just felt right," he says. Lutz is not alone. In my interviews with top executives known for their shrewd business instincts, none could articulate precisely how they routinely made important decisions that defied any logical analysis. To describe that vague feeling of knowing something without knowing exactly how or why, they used words like "professional judgment," "intuition," "gut instinct," "inner voice," and "hunch," but they couldn't describe the process much beyond that.

Our emotions and feelings might not only be important in our intuitive ability to make good decisions but may actually be essential.

Intrigued, I turned to leading scientists who have studied how people make decisions. Although the inner workings of the human mind are a mystery that may never be solved, I found that recent research has uncovered some striking clues suggesting that our emotions and feelings might not only be important in our intuitive ability to make good decisions but may actually be essential. Furthermore, I was told, the type of instinctive genius that enables a CEO to craft the perfect strategy for usurping competitors could require an uncanny ability to detect patterns, perhaps subconsciously, that other people either overlook or mistake for random noise.

So, then, what exactly is your gut and how does it work? When does it tend to be right—and wrong? An explanation of how your intuition works may surprise you; it might even change the way you make decisions. Before that, though, comes a more basic question: why is your gut important in the first place?

An X Factor

Over the years, various management studies have found that executives routinely rely on their intuitions to solve complex problems when logical methods (such as a cost-benefit analysis) simply won't do. In fact, the consensus is that the higher up on the corporate ladder people climb, the more they'll need well-honed business instincts. In other words, intuition is one of the X factors separating the men from the boys.

Ralph S. Larsen, chair and CEO of Johnson & Johnson, explains the distinction: "Very often, people will do a brilliant job up through the middle management levels, where it's very heavily quantitative in terms of the decision-making. But then they reach senior management, where the problems get more complex and ambiguous, and we discover that their judgment or intuition is not what it should be. And when that happens, it's a problem; it's a *big* problem."

What has exacerbated that problem is that many companies now find themselves in increasingly turbulent waters. Thanks to rapid advances in technology (the Internet is a prime example), business models in some markets are changing seemingly overnight and new competitors are emerging from nowhere. "Often there is absolutely no way that you could have the time to thoroughly analyze every one of the options or alternatives available to you," says Larsen. "So you have to rely on your business judgment."

Richard Abdoo, chair and CEO of Wisconsin Energy Corporation, agrees. "As we move to a deregulated marketplace, we don't have this slow process of hearings and review and two years to make a decision. We now have to make decisions in a timely manner. And that means that we process the best information that's available and infer from it and use our intuition to make a decision."

Obviously, gut calls are better suited to some functions (corporate strategy and planning, marketing, public relations, human resources, and research and development) than others (production and operations management and finance). But the top jobs at any organization all require sound business instincts. J&J's Larsen uses an example to explain why: "When someone presents an acquisition proposal to me, the numbers always look terrific: the hurdle rates have been met; the return on investment is wonderful; the growth rate is just terrific. And I get all the reasons why this would be a good acquisition. But it's at that point—when I have a tremendous amount of quantitative information that's already been analyzed by very smart people—that I earn what I get paid. Because I will look at that information and I will know, intuitively, whether it's a good or bad deal."

After 11 years at the helm of J&J, Larsen says that one thing his experience has taught him is to listen to his instincts. "Ignoring them has led to some bad decisions," he notes. Adds Abdoo, "You end up consuming more Rolaids, but you have to learn to trust your intuition. Otherwise, at the point when you've gathered enough data to be 99.99% certain that the decision you're about to make is the correct one, that decision has become obsolete."

Many executives like Lutz, Larsen, and Abdoo have made multimillion-dollar decisions based on their gut instincts. How do they do it? A look at the biological basis of intuition may provide some insights.

What Is Your "Gut"?

Imagine that you're walking in the woods and suddenly come across a large rattlesnake. What happens right before you're consciously aware of the danger? Scientists say that the image of the snake quickly passes from your eyes to your brain, where the information reaches your visual thalamus, which then relays it to your amygdala. A major component of your limbic system, the amygdala then begins sending instructions to your body to increase your heart rate and blood pressure. At this point, though, your visual cortex has yet to confirm that the object you have encountered is indeed a rattlesnake.

Of course, fear is a primal emotion, and the gut instinct that tells a CEO to nix a business deal or promote one vice president over another is a far subtler feeling that is infinitely more complex. But there are two important points.

First, your mind continuously processes information that you are not consciously aware of, not only when you're asleep and dreaming but also when you're awake. This helps explain the "aha" sensation you experience when you learn something that you actually already knew. (This article may be eliciting that very reaction.) Henry Mintzberg, professor of management at McGill University and a longtime proponent of intuitive decision making, says the sense of revelation at the obvious occurs when your conscious mind finally learns something that your subconscious mind had already known. To distinguish between the two kinds of thought, Mintzberg and others have adopted the lay terms "left brain" for the conscious, rational, and logical and "right brain" for the subconscious, intuitive, and emotional. (Although the two terms are gross simplifications of how the human brain actually works, they do provide a convenient shorthand.)

Many executives have learned to tap into their right-brain thinking by jogging, daydreaming, listening to music, or using other meditative techniques. "I get most of my ideas while I'm taking a very long, hot, zoned-out shower in the morning," says Bob Pittman, president of America Online. Pittman also courts his intuitive skills by placing himself in unfamiliar situations. When he was CEO of Six Flags Entertainment, he once worked incognito as a janitor at one of the amusement parks, and on that day he had an epiphany that helped explain why Six Flags was having problems with its janitors being surly to guests. The reason, Pittman realized as he swept the streets, was because management had been ordering the janitors to keep the parks clean, and customers were the ones who were making it dirty. "So we had to go back and redefine their jobs," says Pittman. "We said, 'Your main job isn't to keep the park clean. Your main job is to make sure that people have the greatest day of their lives when they come to Six Flags.' Oh, and by the way, what would prevent customers from enjoying themselves? A dirty park."

Second, your brain is intricately linked to other parts of your body through an extensive nervous system as well as through chemical signals (hormones, neurotransmitters, and modulators). Consequently, some neuroscientists assert that what we call the "mind" is really this intertwined system of brain and body. This, then, helps explain why intuitive feelings are frequently accompanied by physical reactions. When Michael Eisner, CEO of the Walt Disney Company, hears a good idea, for example, he says his body often reacts in a certain way—he sometimes gets an unusual feeling in his stomach, other times in his throat, and other times on his skin. "The sensation is like looking at a great piece of art for the first time," he says.

But how exactly could Eisner's subconscious know that ABC's *Who Wants to Be a Millionaire*—a game show, on prime time, no less—would become a smash hit? In other words, what makes some people's right brain so smart?

The Importance of Being Emotional

Scientists are far from the answer to that question, but recent research has uncovered some provocative clues. Antonio R. Damasio, a leading neuroscientist at the University of Iowa College of Medicine, has been studying people who have suffered brain damage to a specific area in their prefrontal cortices, where we process secondary emotions, such as sorrow aroused through empathy (as opposed to primary emotions, such as fear triggered by the sight of a snake). Such patients retain normal function in many respects—their language and motor skills, attention, memory, intelligence—but they have trouble experiencing certain emotions. When shown photos of people injured in gruesome accidents, for example, they feel nothing.

During his research, Damasio began to notice something peculiar: these patients also had difficulty making simple, even trivial, decisions. In his book *Descartes' Error*, Damasio recounts one particularly bizarre incident in which he asked a patient to choose between two dates for his next appointment. The patient pulled out his engagement book and began going through the myriad reasons for and against each date, taking into consideration his previous commitments, the proximity of them, the possible weather on the two days, and so on. After almost a half hour of listening to this excruciatingly tiresome—yet perfectly rational and logical—analysis, Damasio chose a date for the patient.

To explain this phenomenon, Damasio contends that decision making is far from a cold, analytic process. Instead, says Damasio, our emotions and feelings play a crucial role by helping us filter various possibilities quickly, even though our conscious mind might not be aware of the screening. Our intuitive feelings thus guide our decision making to the point at which our conscious mind is *able* to make good choices. So just as an abundance of emotion (anger, for example) can lead to faulty decisions, so can its paucity.

This point was echoed by Eisner. In my interview with him, he had great difficulty describing how his intuition worked. But when I asked about the possible role of emotions, his response was quick and emphatic: "Balanced emotions are crucial to intuitive decision making," he declared. To explain further, Eisner cited the surrealist painter Marc Chagall's imagery of a horse and man, the former symbolizing our emotions and the latter our rational intellect. "When Chagall drew paintings of a small horse and a giant man," Eisner said, "the horse was too small and couldn't get up on its feet. And when he drew a giant horse, the animal would throw the man off. But when Chagall drew pictures of the horse with the right kind of simpatico with the man—that is, emotions and intellect in balance—then you have instincts that are proper."

A Pattern in Patterns

General intuition is one thing, the business instinct that tells a seasoned venture capitalist whether a start-up will succeed is another. Nobel laureate Herbert A. Simon, a professor of psychology and computer science at Carnegie Mellon University, has studied human decision making for decades and has come to the conclusion that experience enables people to chunk information so that they can store and retrieve it easily. In chess, for instance, Simon found that grand masters are able to recognize and recall perhaps 50,000 significant patterns (give or take a factor of two) of the astronomical number of ways in which the various pieces can be arranged on a board. Associated with that knowledge is important information, such as possible offensive and defensive maneuvers that each cluster of pieces might suggest. "Experts see patterns that elicit from memory the things they know about such situations," says Simon.

AOL's Pittman couldn't agree more. "Staring at market data is like looking at a jigsaw puzzle," he says. "You have to figure out what the picture is. What does it all mean? It's not just a bunch of data. There's a message in there." This is why Pittman routinely loads himself up with as much data as possible. "Every time I get another data point," he explains, "I've added another piece to the jigsaw puzzle, and I'm closer to seeing the answer. And then, one day, the overall picture suddenly comes to me."

In his varied career, Pittman has seen many patterns at work. A cofounder of MTV, he rightly realized when he first arrived at America Online that the company's single most important job was to continue building and establishing its brand—just as it had been for MTV in its early days. Pittman also pushed hard for AOL to continue moving away from a business model based on consumer subscriptions. (Previously, AOL had charged customers by the hour before going to a flat monthly fee.) The bigger bucks, Pittman knew, were in advertising and e-commerce revenues, not in subscriptions. "Most people had been thinking about advertising as money coming out of people's media budgets. I wanted to take a broader view and define advertising as what it really is: renting our consumer relationship to unaffiliated third parties for money." That change in thinking was a masterstroke, enabling AOL to move to a multibillion-dollar revenue stream in just a few years. How could Pittman have intuited that? Perhaps he was influenced by his previous experience at Six Flags Entertainment: the profits from amusement parks derive mainly from selling merchandise and refreshments, not from the admission tickets.

Various studies of experts in diverse fields—parole officers predicting which criminals are likely to break the law again, doctors making diagnoses, school admissions officers predicting which students will succeed, and so on—have confirmed that professional judgment can often be reduced to patterns and rules. In fact, Robyn M. Dawes, a professor in the department of social and decision sciences at Carnegie Mellon University, has uncovered something surprising in his extensive review of these studies: statistical models based on rules typically outperform human experts. For one thing, Dawes says, the models are more consistent: they never suffer from a bad breakfast or a fight with a loved one.

Although little research has examined experts in the business field, several studies confirm Herbert Simon's contention that "intuition and judgment are simply analyses frozen into habit." In one experiment, for example, statistical models using numerous financial ratios (cash flow to total debt, for example) were more accurate in predicting whether a business would fail than bank loan officers making the same judgments. In a different study, statistical models performed as well as two types of retail experts: professional buyers forecasting the catalog sales of different fashion items and brand managers predicting the redemption rate of discount coupons.

According to Simon, when we use our gut, we're drawing on rules and patterns that we can't quite articulate. "All the time," he says, "we are reaching conclusions on the basis of things that go on in our perceptual system, where we're aware of the result of the perception but we're not aware of the steps." Simon claims that intuition is merely those steps, that in-between mechanism that is mysterious only because we don't yet understand how it works. According to him, even extremely sophisticated processes, such as a CEO's deciding whether to acquire a company, can in principle be broken into patterns and rules. "We've been working on expertise of one kind or another since the early 1970s," says Simon, "and wherever we've turned, we found that what distinguishes experts is that they have very good encyclopedias that are indexed, and pattern recognition is that index."

Cross-Indexing

Truly inspired decisions, however, seem to require an even more sophisticated mechanism: *cross*-indexing.

Indeed, the ability to see similar patterns in disparate fields is what elevates a person's intuitive skills from good to sublime.

Remember Bob Lutz's decision to build the Viper? Today, he justifies that gutsy move by using an analogy. "When you're going too slow in an airplane," he explains, "your aerodynamic drag builds up because the nose of the airplane is positioned too high and you can actually get to the point where, even at full power, you can't get the airplane to climb anymore. So your only solution is to drop the nose and trade off some altitude to gain speed." Similarly, Chrysler in the late 1980s had lost so much momentum that it was in danger of stalling. To prevent that, the conventional wisdom called for cost cutting to gain altitude. But Lutz knew better. "People were saying, 'You're low and slow and you're struggling for altitude. What an incredibly bad time to drop the nose and dive some more by spending cash on a frivolous vehicle like the Dodge Viper,'" he remembers. "But the Viper gave us the forward momentum we desperately needed, both internally and externally with the financial community, the automobile magazines, and all of those constituencies that create the psychological climate in which your company either prospers or doesn't."

"In general management, people with varied and diverse backgrounds are, all other things being equal, going to probably be more valuable and will learn faster because they'll recognize more patterns."

Lutz, a former Marine fighter pilot, says that when he first made the gut call to build the Viper, he was not consciously aware that an aerodynamic analogy held the answer to Chrysler's plight. But it's entirely conceivable, he adds, that on a subconscious level his intuition made the connection. "I think I've always had this ability to think laterally," he says. "If I'm learning something specific, I find it very easy to relate it to analogous situations in completely unrelated fields. As long as I understand a basic mechanism, I can usually apply it to a whole lot of other things."

Obviously, the power of cross-indexing increases with the amount of material that can be cross-indexed. Says Lutz, "I find that in general management, people with varied and diverse backgrounds are, all other things being equal, going to probably be more valuable and will learn faster because they'll recognize more patterns." Lutz himself grew up in Europe and has a varied background that is part academic, part military, and part business. Eisner agrees that good intuitive skills must summon the entire mind. "When you see a gas station sign or a certain formation of the clouds," he says, "reams of historical information about yourself that you remember from when you were a child can pop into your mind. Gut instincts are the sum total of those experiences—millions and millions and millions of them. And that sum total enables you to make reasonable decisions."

Know—and Check—Thyself

That said, executives like Lutz and Eisner will be the first to admit that their instincts are often plain wrong. The fact is that various traits of human nature can easily cloud our decision making. For example, we will often take unnecessary risks to recover a loss—the classic gambler's syndrome. Another potential pitfall is our tendency to see patterns where none exist, what statisticians call "overfitting the data."

That our gut instincts are often wrong is exacerbated by the factors that prevent us from realizing just how faulty our intuition can be. First is a tendency toward revisionism: we frequently remember when we didn't trust our gut and should have, while conveniently forgetting when we were fortunate to have ignored our instincts. Then there's the self-fulfilling prophecy: when we hire or promote someone, for instance, we consciously or subconsciously make extra efforts to ensure that person's success, in the end justifying our original decision but obscuring whether our choice was actually a good one.

A dangerous ingredient in this mix is our tendency toward overconfidence. Various surveys have found that we overestimate our ability in just about everything—driving, being able to tell which jokes are funny, distinguishing between European and U.S. handwriting, and so on. Take, for example, our ability to tell when others are lying. Paul Ekman, a professor of psychology at the University of California, San Francisco, has found that we are actually a lot less capable than we think—most of us have only a 50-50 chance of detecting a stranger's lies. The main problem, Ekman says, is that many of us never really find out whether our judgments are accurate, and this lack of feedback is pernicious. If we don't even know we've made mistakes, we can't learn from them, and this blissful ignorance leads us to gain unwarranted confidence in our abilities.

To avoid such pitfalls, many top executives seem to possess a powerful self-checking mechanism. "I am acutely aware of my decisions, and I'm much more aware of the bad decisions that I've made than the good ones," asserts Larsen. Abdoo, the Wisconsin Energy CEO, specifically sets aside about eight hours every week for riding his Harley motorcycle, walking, and working in his basement shop. "During those reflective times," he says, "I often rehash decisions I've made. And when I do, I frequently learn something that helps me when I'm confronted with similar situations in the future."

Such self-assessment can be continual throughout the decision-making process. Says Eisner, "I often sit back and ask myself: why are we doing this, and is it right for the company? Are we making this acquisition for the right reasons, or do we just want some initial good press in the *Wall Street Journal?*" Not coincidentally, Daniel Goleman, a pioneer in the field of emotional intelligence, lists self-awareness—people's ability to recognize their own moods, emotions, and drives—as one of the key criteria for effective leaders.

To see this self-checking mechanism in action, consider how Lutz avoided making a crucial mistake with the Viper project. "When I saw the initial design of the car, I was disappointed because I had expected something that would more closely resemble the original Cobra," he recalls. But soon Lutz became aware that his personal bias for the Cobra was tainting his gut reaction. "I then realized that, much as I liked the Cobra, we couldn't do that car again or it wouldn't have been a Chrysler car," he says. So Lutz in this case went against his instincts and approved the initial design, which became the successful signature look of the Viper.

Because self-checking and feedback are crucial for sound intuitive decisions, some organizations have made these processes part of the culture in executive suites. Top managers at companies like Johnson & Johnson routinely solicit the opinions of others when faced with tough choices. Says Larsen, "Whenever I have this uneasy feeling about a decision we're about to make, for example, about a new product or a major organizational change, I will often ask other trusted advisers who may not have been in the original discussion."

"Don't fall in love with your decisions. Everything's fluid. You have to constantly, subtly make and adjust your decisions."

The goal is to get to the root of the decision maker's uneasiness. "Then all of a sudden," he says, "the light goes on." And this is why, Larsen adds, "in our senior management group, we say we don't really make decisions, we *extrude* them."

But perhaps the greatest power of intuitive decision making coupled with continual feedback is that the process can be honed into an effective management style for quick action. Pittman is a leading practitioner. "Probably more than half of my decisions are wrong," he explains. "But if I have quick decision making, when I inevitably make the wrong decision, I can quickly change it to something else. And, therefore, over time I will have more right decisions working in our business than wrong ones." For example, Pittman might take a particular course of action based on certain assumptions (perhaps a pattern he thinks he sees); but he'll quickly change that decision when new information contradicts some of those assumptions (that is, perhaps the "pattern" really wasn't a pattern after all). Pittman, who is expected to assume a key position in the scheduled merged operations of AOL and media giant Time Warner, has this final piece of advice, culled from his years of experience in making gut calls: "Don't fall in love with your decisions. Everything's fluid. You have to constantly, subtly make and adjust your decisions."

Since my interview with Pittman and other executives, I have found myself trying to make and tweak decisions quickly based on my gut feel. And I no longer attempt to squelch my emotions during the process, although I vigilantly strive to discern the underlying reasons for those feelings. Even with little practice, I do think I have become slightly better at making smart choices, and I strongly believe that people can substantially increase their decision-making prowess by tapping more into the right brain. Interestingly, though, my gut tells me that I will more than likely never reach the kind of intuitive genius that led Lutz to build an outrageous, expensive sports car when conventional logic dictated otherwise. But, then, perhaps this helps explain why so many companies fail to build Vipers when they need to, because not every executive is blessed with the exquisite instincts of a Bob Lutz.

Originally published in February 2001
Reprint R0102C

About the Contributors

CHRIS ARGYRIS is the James Conant Professor Emeritus of Education and Organizational Behavior at Harvard University. He has consulted to numerous private and governmental organizations. He has received many awards including 11 honorary degrees and Lifetime Contribution Awards from the Academy of Management, American Psychological Association, and American Society of Training Directors. His most recent books are *Flawed Advice* and *On Organizational Learning*. He is currently Director of Monitor Group.

PETER F. DRUCKER is a writer, teacher, and consultant whose 32 books have been published in more than 20 languages. He is cofounder of the Peter F. Drucker Foundation for Nonprofit Management and has counseled numerous governments, businesses, and public service institutions.

AMITAI ETZIONI served as the Ford Foundation Professor at Harvard Business School from 1987–89. He is the author of *Modern Organizations*, *The Moral Dimensions: Toward a New Economics*, and *The Limits of Privacy*. He served as Senior Adviser to the White House and as the President of the American Sociology Association. He taught at Columbia University for 20 years and is currently a University Professor at The George Washington University. He can be reached by e-mail at etzioni@gwu.edu.

JOHN S. HAMMOND is an internationally known consultant, speaker, and author, and is a former professor at the Harvard Business School. He is coauthor of the award-winning best seller, *Smart Choices: A Practical Guide to Making Better Decisions*, which has been translated into a dozen languages. He is also coauthor of *Management Decision Sciences, Strategic Market Planning*, and many articles including four in *Harvard Business Review*. Founder of John S. Hammond & Associates in Lincoln, MA, his current practice focuses on helping managers make tough strategic decisions and plan major negotiations. He also provides customized training in negotiation skills.

ALDEN M. HAYASHI is a Senior Editor with *Harvard Business Review*. He has more than 15 years of publishing experience covering science and high technology. Before joining *HBR*, he was a member of the Board of Editors for *Scientific American*, where he wrote and edited articles on computer science, physics, and mathematics. He was also Executive Editor of *Datamation*, a monthly computer trade magazine for information-technology professionals.

RALPH L. KEENEY is a Professor at the University of Southern California in the Marshall School of Business and the School of Engineering, and is affiliated with the Center for Telecommunications Management. He also has a private consulting practice, based in San Francisco, where his clients include American Express, British Columbia Hydro, Fair Isaac, Kaiser Permanente, Pacific Gas & Electric, and Seagate Technology. He is especially known for his work on making difficult decisions involving multiple objectives. Dr. Keeney is the author of several books including *Value-Focused Thinking: A Path to Creative Decision-Making* and *Decisions with Multiple Objectives*, coauthored with Howard Raiffa. Dr. Keeney was previously a professor at MIT and is a member of the National Academy of Engineering.

Professor Emeritus and decision analyst **HOWARD RAIFFA** was a member of the Harvard faculty from 1957–1994, when he retired. His main affiliation was with the business school, but he also held joint appointments with the departments of statistics and economics and gave courses in several other schools at Harvard. He was one of the founding members and a faculty member of the Kennedy School of Government. He helped negotiate the creation of the International Institute for Systems Analysis, located in Vienna, Austria, and from 1972–1975 was the first director. He holds several honorary doctorates and was the year 2000 recipient of the Dickson Prize for Science, conferred by Carnegie Mellon University for his lifetime accomplishments in game theory, statistical decision theory, decision analysis, societal risk analysis, and in the art and science of negotiations.

At the time this article was originally published, **PERRIN STRYKER** was the author of numerous articles on various aspects of management. For many years he was an editor of *Fortune*, and, before that, he wrote for *Newsweek*.

Index

Abdoo, Richard, 174–175, 184–185
abstractions, 17–19
acceptable versus "right" decisions, 3, 11–13
action commitment, 3, 13–17. *See also* words versus actions
  human capacities and, 2, 13, 14–15
  who needs to know and, 2, 13–14
adaptive techniques, 54–57. *See also* mixed scanning
"aha" sensation, 175–176
alternatives. *See also* even-swap method
  elimination of, 25–29
  identification of, 151
America Online, 176, 179–180. *See also* Pittman, Bob
anchoring trap, 143, 146–149
antagonism, 63, 78–81
automobile industry, 7–8

Bay of Pigs decision, 11

behavior changes
  human capabilities and, 15–17
  interpersonal barriers and, 81–92
Bell Telephone System, 16
blind alleys, 82–84
blind spots, 76–78
boundary conditions, 3, 9–13
burred-quarter-panel problem. *See also* Kepner-Tregoe approach
  background situation in, 98–111, 114–115
  executive dilemma in, 110–111
  personnel involved in, 92–93, 114–115
  problem analysis for, 115–141
business instincts. *See also* intuition
  importance in top jobs, 173–175
  Lutz and, 172
  pattern recognition and, 179–181

Chagall, Marc, 178–179
change, as basic cause of problems, 133–136
changing decisions
  reversible decisions and, 56–57
  shift in goals and, 10
Chrysler Corporation, 182–183. *See also* Lutz, Bob
  Cobra, 170–171, 185
  Dodge Viper, 171–172, 182–183, 185
classification, 3–7
commitment
  to action, 3, 13–17
  escalation of, 153
  restricted, 67–69
communication, 17–19. *See also* interpersonal barriers
compromises, right versus wrong, 2, 11–13
confirming-evidence trap, 143–144, 155–157
conformity, 63, 80
conscious versus subconscious thought, 175–177. *See also* psychological traps
consequences table, 24–25. *See also* even-swap method
consistency, 40
consultation with others
  interpersonal barriers and, 84
  psychological traps and, 148, 149, 161
controls, and human relationships, 65, 80, 83–84

cost-benefit analysis
  exaggeration of costs and, 152
  worst-case analysis and, 164
"counsels of despair," 50–51
counterarguments, 156–157
cross-indexing, 181–183
Cuban missile crisis, 6
culture
  interpersonal barriers and, 64–65, 74
  sunk-cost trap and, 153–155

Damasio, Antonio R., 177–179
data. *See* information
Dawes, Robyn M., 180
decision-making process. *See also* even-swap method; interpersonal barriers
  action commitment and, 3
  classification and, 2, 3–7
  problem definition, 3, 7–9, 118–122
  "right" versus acceptable solutions, 3, 11–13
  sequence of steps in, 2–3
  specification of goals, 3, 9–11
  validity testing and, 3, 17–19
decision staggering, 55
decision traps. *See* psychological traps
Descartes' Error (Damasio), 178
devil's advocate, 156–157
direction, and human relationships, 65

distrust, 78–81
dominated alternatives, 25–29

effectiveness. *See also* interpersonal barriers
 emotions as blocks to, 65
 factors in, 60–62
 feedback and, 3, 17–19
 organizational defenses and, 81
 quick action and, 1
Eisner, Michael, 177, 185
Ekman, Paul, 184
emotional intelligence, 185
emotions. *See also* psychological traps
 expression of, 62
 pitfalls and, 49
 role in decision making, 177–179
 suppression of, 65, 66
estimating traps, 161–166
even-swap method, 21–44
 Benjamin Franklin's approach and, 42–44
 complex decision example, 32, 33–37
 concept behind, 29–30
 consequences table and, 24–25
 dominated alternatives and, 25–29
 franchising decision example, 30–32
 guidelines for using, 37–41
 nature of system, 23–24
 steps in, 30–32

executive behavior patterns, 61–62, 63. *See also* interpersonal barriers
 consequences of, 62–64, 67–81
 contradictory statements and, 74–76
 inadequate approaches to, 81–84
 lack of awareness of, 72–76
 words versus actions and, 60–62

Federal Reserve, 55
feedback
 effectiveness and, 3, 17–19
 interpersonal barriers and, 84–85, 87–91
flexibility, 60
focused trial and error, 54
forecasting traps, 161–166
fractionalizing, 55–56
framing trap, 144, 157–161
Franklin, Benjamin, 42–44
future impacts, and status-quo trap, 152

gains versus losses, and framing, 158–159
gambling, 11, 183
General Motors Corporation, 9–10, 12. *See also* Sloan, Alfred P., Jr.
generic events
 apparent uniqueness and, 4–5

generic events (*continued*)
   new generic events and,
      5–6
   true generic events, 3–4
   versus truly unique events, 5
goals. *See also* culture
   specification of, 3, 9–11
   status-quo trap and, 151
go-for-it approach, 50–51
Goleman, Daniel, 185
group process. *See also* inter-
      personal barriers
   attention to, 64–65, 85–87
   decisions introduced by
      executive and, 67–69
   negative presentations and,
      70–72

hedging bets, 56
heuristics, 144–145. *See also*
      psychological traps
human capabilities
   action commitment and, 2,
      13, 14–15
   behavior changes and, 15–17
human mind. *See also* psycho-
      logical traps
   conscious versus subcon-
      scious thought and,
      175–177
   heuristic routines and,
      144–145
   limits of, 48–49
human relationships, in execu-
      tive values, 64–65. *See also*
      interpersonal barriers

humble decision making
      model, 45–47, 52. *See also*
      mixed scanning
hunches, 130–131, 137

incentives
   action commitment and,
      15–17
   human relationships and, 65
incrementalism, 45, 50, 52–53
information
   in even-swap method, 40–41
   interpersonal barriers and,
      78–81, 85–87
   versus knowledge, 48
   patterns in market data and,
      179
   undependable, 51
interpersonal barriers, 59–65
   antagonism and, 78–81
   bad approaches to, 81–84
   blind alleys and, 82–84
   blind spots and, 76–78
   consequences of executive
      behaviors and, 62–64,
      67–81
   damaged processes and, 81
   distrust and, 78–81
   executive lack of awareness
      of, 72–76
   feedback utilization and,
      87–91
   group involvement and,
      85–87
   influence of values on opera-
      tions and, 65–66

laboratory training and, 91–92

pattern A behaviors and, 61

pattern B behaviors and, 61–62

restricted commitment and, 67–69

six-company study on, 59–60, 93–95

subordinate gamesmanship and, 70–72

tape-recording of meetings and, 87–91

value of questions and, 84–85

words versus actions and, 60–62

intuition. *See also* business instincts

cross-indexing and, 181–183

emotions and, 177–179

feedback and, 184, 185–186

making trade-offs and, 21, 23

physiological basis of, 175–177

pitfalls of, 50–51, 183–187

quick action and, 186

self-checking and, 184–187

Johnson & Johnson, 173, 185–186. *See also* Larsen, Ralph S.

Kennedy Administration policies, 6, 11

Kepner, Charles H., 98

Kepner-Tregoe approach. *See also* burred-quarter-panel problem

change as cause of problems and, 133–136

problem definition and, 118–122

relevant distinctions and, 126–133, 138, 139, 140

respecification of problem and, 136–141

specification worksheet and, 122–126, 127, 135–136

stair-stepping process in, 120–121, 122

testing possible causes and, 135–136

knowledge. *See also* information

versus information, 48

partial, and adaptive techniques, 54–57

laboratory training, and interpersonal barriers, 91–92

Larsen, Ralph S., 173–174, 175, 184, 186

lectures, and behavior change, 82

left brain thinking, 176

Lutz, Bob, 170–172, 175, 182–183, 185, 187

market data, patterns in, 179

medical decision making, 45, 46, 53, 54

memory, and psychological traps, 164–165
mergers, 151
Mintzberg, Henry, 175–176
mistakes. *See also* psychological traps
  admission of, 154
  incomplete problem definition and, 7–9
  problem classification and, 6–7
mixed scanning
  adaptive techniques in, 54–57
  humble decision making model and, 45–47, 52
  incrementalism and, 50, 52–53
  non-rational approaches and, 50–52
  rationalism and, 47–50, 52–53
  types of judgments in, 52–53

Northeastern blackout, 7

objectives. *See* goals
openness
  emotions and, 66
  interpersonal barriers and, 92
  to others' ideas, 63
  reasons for changes and, 78–81
organizational defenses, 81. *See also* interpersonal barriers

overconfidence, 144, 162–163, 165–166, 184

pattern A behaviors, 61
pattern B behaviors, 61–62
pattern recognition, 179–181
performance measurement, 16
pitfalls. *See also* psychological traps
  human factors and, 49–50
  incompatible goal specifications, 10–11
  reliance on intuition and, 50–51, 183–187
Pittman, Bob, 176, 179–180, 186
political factors, 49
practical dominance, 27, 28
principles
  generic events and, 5–6
  mistaken application of, 6–7
probability assessments, 164–165
problem definition. *See also* framing trap
  in decision-making process, 3, 7–9
  decisions versus problems and, 118, 119
  different perspectives and, 148
  Kepner-Tregoe approach and, 118–122
  reframing and, 160
procrastination, 55

prudence trap, 144, 163–164, 166

psychological traps, 143–167. *See also* human mind
  anchoring trap, 143, 146–149
  avoidance of, 144, 146, 148–149, 151–152, 154–155, 156–157, 160–161, 165–166
  combinations of, 166–167
  confirming-evidence trap, 143–144, 155–157
  estimating traps, 161–166
  forecasting traps, 161–166
  framing trap, 144, 157–161
  overconfidence trap, 144, 162–163, 165–166
  prudence trap, 144, 163–164, 166
  recallability trap, 144, 164–165, 166
  status-quo trap, 143, 149–152
  sunk-cost trap, 143, 152–155

questions, value of, 84–85

rationalism, 45. *See also* even-swap method
  executive values regarding, 65
  limitations of, 47–50, 52–53
rational ritualism, 51
recallability trap, 144, 164–165, 166

reference points, and framing, 159–160
relative value, 39–40
reversible decisions, 56–57
revisionism, 184
right brain thinking, 176
risk-taking, 60–61, 62, 66
Roosevelt, Franklin D., 10

self-awareness
  "binds" in group process and, 88–89
  emotional intelligence and, 185
  executive lack of, 72–76
  psychological traps and, 144, 146, 167
self-checking, 184–187
self-fulfilling prophecy, 184
sensory misperceptions, 145. *See also* psychological traps
Simon, Herbert A., 179, 181
Six Flags Entertainment, 176, 180
Sloan, Alfred P., Jr., 9–10, 12
statistical models, 181
status-quo trap, 143, 149–152
strategic reserves, maintenance of, 56
subjectivity, 40–41. *See also* intuition
subordinates
  confusion and, 77
  gamesmanship and, 70–72

subordinates (*continued*)
  interpersonal barriers and,
    70–72, 77–78, 86–87
  sunk-cost trap and, 154
  unwritten rules and, 71–72
sunk-cost trap, 143, 152–155

tentativeness, 54–55
trade-offs, 21–44. *See also*
    even-swap method
  canceling objectives and,
    29–32
  elimination of alternatives
    in, 25–29

picturing alternatives in,
    24–25
Tregoe, Benjamin B., 98
trust, 60, 80
  distrust and, 78–81

uncertainty, and rational
    approaches, 47–48

Vail, Theodore, 16

words versus actions, 60–62